04

what's the ALTERNATIVE?

Career Options for Librarians and Info Pros

Rachel Singer Gordon

 **Information Today, Inc.**
Medford, New Jersey

First printing, 2008

What's the Alternative? Career Options for Librarians and Info Pros

Library of Congress Cataloging-in-Publication Data

Gordon, Rachel Singer.
   What's the alternative?. : career options for librarians and info pros / Rachel Singer Gordon.
      p. cm.
   Includes bibliographical references and index.
   ISBN 978-1-57387-333-8
   1. Library science--Vocational guidance--United States. 2. Information science--Vocational guidance--United States. I. Title.
   Z682.35.V62G68 2008
   020.23--dc22

                                                                2008005972

Printed and bound in the United States of America

President and CEO: Thomas H. Hogan, Sr.
Editor-in-Chief and Publisher: John B. Bryans
Managing Editor: Amy M. Reeve
VP Graphics and Production: M. Heide Dengler
Book Designer: Kara Mia Jalkowski
Cover Designer: Michael Hardwick
Copyeditor: Beverly Michaels
Proofreader: Pat Hadley-Miller
Indexer: Sharon Hughes

www.infotoday.com

Contents

Chapter 7: Working in Very Different Roles

Chapter 8: Working in IT Outside of Libraries

Chapter 9: Nontraditional Roles, Traditional Institutions

Acknowledgments

This book was only made possible through the stories of many info pros who have forged alternative paths. Their willingness to share their experiences and insights reflects librarians' innate commitment to collaboration and sharing information. Through quotes and sidebars, I've attempted to represent their comments in the spirit intended—responsibility for any misinterpretation lies with me alone. I also continue to rely on the support of the Editor-in-Chief at Information Today, Inc., John Bryans, and the rest of the dedicated folks in the Book Publishing Division. As always, my family's unwavering patience and support have been invaluable: A big thank you to Todd, Jacob, and Samuel for just being yourselves!

About the Web Page

This book references a number of online resources useful to those moving into a wide variety of nontraditional careers (see Appendix C for a list of URLs by chapter). Instead of typing numerous URLs into your Web browser, please visit this book's companion Web site at www.lisjobs.com/altcareers, where you'll find a clickable link to each site mentioned in the text. Since Web pages tend to come and go, in order to make *What's the Alternative?* more useful and enduring to its readers, the addresses for the online resources will be kept updated on this Web site.

Please feel free to email any changes, comments, and suggestions to rachel@lisjobs.com.

Disclaimer

Neither the publisher nor the author makes any claim as to the results that may be obtained through the use of this Web site or of any of the Internet resources it references or links to. Neither publisher nor author will be held liable for any results, or lack thereof, obtained by the use of this page or any of its links; for any third-party changes; or for any hardware, software, or other problems that may occur as the result of using it. This Web site is subject to change or discontinuation without notice at the discretion of the publisher and author.

Foreword

Rachel Singer Gordon has been on my "must read" list ever since I came across a column she had written as a NextGen contributor to *Library Journal.* Her column was thoughtful, articulate, engaging, and—although it clearly represented a specific generational viewpoint—inclusive. Very much like this book. The column also pointed out that in order to move forward in a positive way, we *all* needed to consider a broader encompass for how we approached librarianship as a profession. Again, very much like this book.

As Rachel points out, librarianship as a profession is in the midst of tremendous transition. For a host of reasons—often tied to budgets, technologies, and changing expectations—many traditional library jobs are going away or being de-professionalized. However, *What's the Alternative? Career Options for Librarians and Info Pros* makes the point that alternative LIS career choices and potential career paths are now continually expanding to encompass new skills, new knowledge, new generational viewpoints, and myriad new opportunities.

So how do you get started in this brave new LIS world? By reading this book. *What's the Alternative?* provides you with a wonderfully rich collection of ideas, information, and resources that lays out the landscape of alternative careers. Chapter by chapter, the book walks you through types of potential careers, the pros and cons of those career choices, and the knowledge and experience you'll need to succeed. In addition, the book offers practical and wise strategies for moving your career forward at your own pace, and based on your individual circumstances.

Equally valuable, *What's the Alternative?* presents the personal stories—in their own words—of LIS professionals who've made the very types of transitions described. Dozens of professionals who've made "alternative" career choices talk about the reality of those choices, bringing the theoretical "there are lots of options" into the realm of "and here's what those options really look like." More than 100 profiles, interviews, and quotes interwoven throughout provide the detail necessary to bring life to individual career choices. Although this is valuable for all of us, it's especially helpful for students who may have little practical knowledge of what various jobs entail.

"Why place limits on yourself and what you can do?" the book asks, and then proceeds to explain how you can move well beyond any limits the profession or your own hesitation might impose. Part of that process is understanding that, as Rachel states, "careers tend not to last forever, and you need not feel permanently locked into whatever path you choose. The shifting nature of information work, personal exigencies, and expanding opportunities all mean that info pros now shift between alternative careers and more traditional environments more easily and frequently than in the past. ... Keep your options open and retain your connections to the profession, because you never know what the future may hold."

That wise attitude is why, when I teach a course every spring for the University of Denver MLIS program on alternative career paths, I always have Rachel Singer Gordon on the short list of writers for my students to keep an eye on. I like the way she thinks, and I'm always interested in whatever she's thinking about. Happily for all of us, she's been thinking about the future of library and information work here. And once again, her writing is thoughtful, articulate, engaging, and inclusive.

So do yourself a favor and find a comfortable chair, a pen, and your favorite cup of coffee or tea. Then sit down and start exploring your bright future of professional possibilities.

Kim Dority, MLS
Author, *Rethinking Information Work: A Career Guide
for Librarians and Other Information Professionals*

Introduction

*Entering a profession because it looks promising
or secure is the ultimate crapshoot. ... Even more
damaging to our vocational development is the
belief that work is nothing more than a way to
earn money. Why should we commit a third—or
more—of our time to doing something that we
don't care about? Why can't we get paid for being
happy?[1]*

People have traditionally gone into librarianship with the sense
that they are entering a fairly stable profession, most never intending, at least at the outset, to take their library skills to a nontraditional field. There has, however, been a longstanding interest in
alternative options, as borne out by a small flurry of books and
articles on the subject from the mid-1980s through the mid-90s. (A
number of these are listed in Appendix D.) Now, technological
advances, changes in library school education, and changes in the
way our society views information work all serve to make alternative careers both more attractive and less "alternative" than they
once were. Nontraditional career opportunities for info pros continue to expand, as organizations of all sizes realize the need to
store, retrieve, and organize their information, and as librarians
realize their ability to retool and transfer their skills. Those librarians and information professionals who can capitalize on these
trends and utilize their skills in nontraditional ways can maximize
their career options. *What's the Alternative?* explores some of these
possibilities.

Running through these chapters is the underlying thread of
transferable skills. Librarians and info pros in all types of institutions can easily apply their skills, background, and expertise to
new environments, allowing us to think of information work more

broadly than just "jobs in libraries." What else can you do with a library degree or library experience? The facile answer is: just about anything! The thoughtful answer is: anything that uses both your skills and knowledgebase (including both your info pro skills and your additional abilities), and feeds your soul. In these pages, other info pros discuss some of the better fits they have found, but be sure to look at these options as suggestions for potential directions, rather than as a list of limited possibilities.

While you will read quite a bit here on alternative full-time career paths, you will also discover options for part-time, patchwork, or freelance nontraditional work, as well as nontraditional careers within libraries themselves. This book also discusses when, how, and why to make the jump to another field, and recommends organizations, resources, and support networks for those who are striking out on their own.

Chapter 1 talks about making the leap to an alternative career, discussing how best to make that decision and create a plan for a productive career path. Chapter 2 then suggests ways to ease into a career transition by taking a position in an organization that serves libraries and/or librarians, while Chapter 3 pushes just a bit further, talking about opportunities in organizations similar to libraries.

Chapter 4 invites you to take the plunge into self-employment, with a discussion of various ways to strike out on your own. This chapter also contains a discussion of "multiple profit centers," with the idea that we as info pros don't need to limit or define ourselves by a single type of work. Chapter 5 continues the self-employment theme, with information on building a business, entrepreneurship, info brokering, and becoming your own vendor.

In Chapter 6, read about continuing to work with information in nontraditional roles or in nontraditional institutions. Then, jump into Chapter 7, which talks about very different roles that you may not expect. Chapter 8 may start you thinking about working in an information technology role outside of a library.

Chapter 9 covers nontraditional roles in traditional institutions, and explores some of the ways in which our changing field is opening up new opportunities while allowing us to remain close to home. In Chapter 10, come back into the fold, with a discussion on moving back to traditional librarianship from an alternative career, and the opportunities and pitfalls this decision presents. Lastly, Chapter 11 takes a look at where we might go from here, and the appendixes offer some additional resources, including advice on finding nontraditional jobs, a survey on alternative careers, a list of Web sites referenced, and a number of other resources for further exploration.

Whether you are a long-term librarian thinking of pursuing a different path post-retirement, a mid-career librarian experiencing burnout and feeling the need to do something different, an entry-level librarian having trouble breaking into the field, or a non-MLS library worker seeking broader opportunities, the stories and suggestions in these chapters should help spark ideas for your own alternative career. (I use the terms *librarian* and *information professional* throughout, but most of these career paths are open to all library workers and info pros, with or without an MLS.) While no book on nontraditional jobs can be comprehensive—after all, you can use your skills as an info pro to pursue just about *any* career—you will find discussions of some of the most commonly pursued options and thoughts on how your skills may best transfer.

You'll also read stories and hear advice and ideas from people working in a variety of nontraditional fields. Respondents to an online survey on alternative careers (see Appendix B) are quoted and their stories highlighted in sidebars throughout. Their willingness to share their experiences highlights the collaborative and giving nature of our profession, no matter where our individual career paths may take us.

My interest in alternative careers stems from my own unplanned career detour. After working in public libraries for 10 years, I'm now self-employed, stitching together multiple threads to create a personal career path outside of, yet still related to, libraries. I wish you the best of luck as you forge your own path!

Rachel Singer Gordon
rachel@lisjobs.com

Endnotes

1. Barbara J. Winter, *Making a Living Without a Job: Winning Ways for Creating Work That You Love,* New York: Bantam, 1993: 10.

Chapter 1

Making the Leap

The truth is, you can't find a job that's a life sentence anymore, even if you're looking for one. ... Many people ... find it best to carry their skills with them like a plumber carries his tools.[1]

The decision to make the leap from libraries to nontraditional work, or to launch a post-MLS career in an alternative field, is very personal. Each of us has to choose the best career path for our own skills and needs, realizing that no job is forever and no path set in stone. More and more often, people choose to pursue multiple careers throughout their working lives rather than to pledge undying loyalty to a single employer or profession; U.S. workers now average five different occupations over the course of their working life. As our needs, interests, skill sets, and the very environment around us continue to evolve, the ways in which we contribute must change as well. Sometimes we change and outgrow the job we're in; sometimes the job itself changes so that it no longer fits us. Why not do something different?

Many librarians spend some time easing into an alternative career, taking on freelance projects or a part-time job while still employed full time in a traditional library. (This route can lead to potential conflicts of interest, though, especially if you jump into consulting or other freelance work directly related to your current job.) Some combine careers indefinitely, expanding their horizons and/or pocketbooks in various ways while still retaining the stability of regular employment. Others make the jump decisively, without once looking back. And an increasing number of information professionals jump directly into an alternative field post-graduation. *Library Journal's* October 2006 placement and salaries report on 2005 LIS graduates showed 10.5 percent of respondents working in the "other" category, many emphasizing that they still use their librarian skills and competencies to succeed, while its October 2007 article on 2006 grads reported a 43.7 percent jump from the previous year in the number of LIS grads employed outside the profession.[2]

If you do plan to ease into an alternative career with the goal of eventually exiting the library environment entirely, then commit to do so and set goals: What will you accomplish in one year? In five years? Create a realistic strategy for transitioning into your new career. Otherwise, admit that you are just dabbling in other options or taking a side job. That's fine, too; each of us has to choose the path that's right for us. The people quoted and interviewed in these pages have each taken an individual path; use their stories to inspire you to forge your own.

Who Should Leap?

The decision to transition to an alternative career often depends more on opportunity and outside factors than on an innate desire to make the jump. People have many reasons for moving outside the traditional library field. You might investigate alternative work because:

- As a new grad or other entry-level candidate, you find that traditional avenues are closed to you due to a tight job market or your lack of geographic mobility, so you wish either to switch fields entirely or pursue a related career until a traditional position opens up.

- You lack an MLS and want to explore options that use your library experience but offer greater opportunity for advancement than available to you at most traditional institutions.

- As a retiring librarian, you now have the opportunity to pursue lifelong dreams or enter new fields; or, as a librarian close to or contemplating retirement, you're looking for the answer to what to do with the rest of your life.

- Your library is shutting its doors or downsizing, and you feel the need to look for alternative—and perhaps more stable—employment.

- You want to explore freelance or part-time options in addition to your current traditional library work, either to supplement your income or to stimulate your brain.

- You are seeking more flexibility or better work-life balance, due to childcare or other issues, and want to investigate part-time options, flexible work, 9-to-5 work, and/or work that can be done from home.

- You want to find options that use your skills as an information professional while providing better compensation or other benefits than traditional library work.

- You enter an LIS program or school of information with an appreciation for the skills and knowledge you can acquire, but with no intention of ever working in a traditional library position.

- You fall into an alternative career and find that the work suits your abilities and temperament.

- A major life event changes your perspective on your career and your path, inspiring you to pursue new dreams.

- You want more opportunities to use your creativity and feel stifled by traditional library bureaucracy; you're bored and need new challenges.

- You crave the independence of working for yourself, or you have a strong entrepreneurial streak.

- Your current library position offers insufficient opportunities for growth and/or personal satisfaction, and you fear a lateral move may offer more of the same.

- You find that your idealized picture of library work fails to match its reality; you find that you are unable in a real-world environment to put your principles into practice; you find that the actuality of real-world library work fails to match your initial expectations; you want to explore options that better fit your earlier hopes.

- You are unhappy every day at work.

Think about what might motivate you, be it one or more of these common reasons, or reasons not even listed here. Determining your motivation for leaving the library field can help you determine your path, and can help you decide whether you truly wish to leave libraries, or just your *particular* library. You might even move on simply because you have absorbed what you can from your current job and want to explore new challenges. Mark Larson, Web Content Analyst, HowStuffWorks.com, Atlanta, GA, explains: "I'm still young yet, so I didn't feel like I had to make library work fit, and didn't have much to lose by leaving. I wasn't stressed about 'the leap.' I gave a good commitment, learned a lot, and moved on."

Thinking ahead also helps you prepare for unexpected changes and challenges. If you are downsized, defunded, or find yourself having to relocate unexpectedly, you will be in a better position to move on if you have already given thought to other options. Cynthia J. Coan, self-employed indexer, Indexing By the Book,

Tucson, AZ, says: "In view of life's unpredictability and the possibility of major changes in one's job situation, it is always wise to have a backup plan. As a test, ask yourself: If I couldn't stay in the library field, where would I turn for employment?"

Open your mind and expand your options—while you can obviously explore other careers in traditional libraries, why limit yourself? Why not also explore moving beyond traditional library work? If your current library job or your LIS program fails to fulfill you in one way or another, be willing to stretch yourself and to imagine the type of work that will bring you joy. This may be as simple as moving to another type of library, a healthier library, or another type of position within libraries, or as dramatic as embarking on an entirely new career. As Julie Jansen writes, "Living is about making choices. Deciding what kind of work will make you happy is a choice, a big one. Today there are so many choices that sometimes it may seem easier to sit still and not make any at all. But you have a clear choice—you can either decide to begin the process of change, or you can continue doing something that isn't making you happy."[3]

Most important here is the idea that this is a process. You can certainly keep your day job while also beginning to stretch your wings in other directions; you can keep looking for a library job in your chosen field and geographical area while simultaneously investigating alternative careers to pay the bills in the meantime. A willingness to explore options and to not get locked into either/or will go a long way toward building a fulfilling career. At the same time, creating a plan will help you avoid dithering away your working years while failing to commit to the path you know in your heart you want to follow. If you seek a change, take the time to outline the steps you need to take to get to where you want to be.

Keep your resume updated and look out for opportunities to stretch your skills. Follow the job market and the growth of nontraditional opportunities, and think about ways you can gain the skills these types of employers seek. Look at your peers and the type of work they do; think about whether you might find it interesting. As Jen Doyle, Director of Curriculum and Communications, Simmons College GSLIS, Boston, says: "Go with what interests you! Find out as much as possible about what everyone you know does so that you can figure out what works for you." Always be in touch with whether your current position continues to stretch you professionally and engage you personally, and stay open to both traditional and nontraditional possibilities. Keep an eye out, keep your skills up, and keep yourself mentally prepared for making a move. Not sure if you really want to make the leap? Start with a little quiz on job and career change from Quintessential Careers (www.quintcareers.com/career_change_quiz.html).

Adjusting Attitudes

For many of us, the decision to move to an alternative environment involves a great deal of soul-searching. This can be a wrenching decision, especially if you originally went into the profession with specific goals, because you wanted to make a difference, or because the field seemed to match your personal values and beliefs. Some view moving to another field as literally abandoning the profession, after working so hard to get the MLS or making a years-long commitment to libraries. Others feel librarianship to be a true vocation, or treasure the principles of the profession. They fear that, by leaving, they will either lose something of themselves or lose the chance to make the same impact on their communities. Librarians often choose the profession because they find meaning in their work, although the source of this meaning differs for each of us.

There's no single right answer here—we all have to make our own decisions about our individual career paths. If you are contemplating an alternative career because of poor job prospects, poor pay, or poor management in your own institution, yet still feel attached to librarianship as a field or believe that library work has special significance, you might start by investigating employment that is in some way related to library work. Sit down and take some time to identify the exact aspects of the profession that are important to you. Do you want to help people? Do you love research and tracking down information? Do you thrive on working with the public? Are you committed to literacy or to intellectual freedom, or do you need to be around books all day? Is it important that you remain in the public sector? Would volunteering in a library or a similar institution be enough, or do you want your primary career to be library focused?

Determining your personal priorities and passions will help ensure that you carry over these principles to a new career. If literacy and education are key, you can look into related jobs such as teaching, working with literacy organizations, or tutoring. If helping people is key, you can think about working for a charity or a nonprofit organization. If you just love being around books, why not look at jobs in bookstores, think about starting your own rare bookselling business, or comb garage sales, thrift stores, and library book sales—mobile Web in hand—to find stacks of titles to sell on Amazon or eBay?

If you are making the jump to another field because of negative reasons—say, you couldn't find a professional job post-graduation, your company downsized you, your organization eliminated its library—even more adjustment will be required. You need to shift your thinking to see this as an opportunity—yes, easier said than done, but dwelling on your predicament is less than productive, and your loss can be the catalyst for a new career. Any change holds the seeds of opportunity. Move forward rather than dwelling on what might have been.

Moving outside the box of traditional librarianship is a life-changing decision, and one of your goals here can be to establish, or re-establish, the best possible fit between work and self. Those who choose to move from public, school, or academic librarianship to private sector work with a vendor or other for-profit company should also realize the need to adjust their expectations of the work environment and their attitude toward the goal of making a profit. This issue will be discussed in more detail in later chapters, but recognize that working environments and organizational goals in non-library fields may differ greatly from what you are used to. Take the time to create a realistic picture of your potential future career and research your options before making the leap.

Assessing Values

While some fall into an alternative career, others plan for it—or at least plan for the type of future that may include alternatives. One way to begin planning your *career* as an information professional, rather than simply following "the next job," is to honestly assess your personal values as they pertain to work. Begin by making a list of the types of things you are looking for in your next career. Include both tangible and intangible benefits, which could comprise factors such as:

- Autonomy
- Challenge
- Diversity
- Fast pace
- Flexibility
- Focus on people
- Focus on technology
- Opportunity for advancement
- Security

- Sufficient compensation

- Work/life balance

Ask yourself a series of questions to help hone in on what you want out of your next job: Are you looking to move into management? Make a certain amount of money? Move near family? Strike out on your own? Find a career path that stimulates you intellectually or feeds your soul? Build more balance into your life? Are you looking for stable employment, or do you thrive on change or ambiguity? What motivates you to do your best work? Respect? Money? Prestige? Feeling that you are making a difference? What do you value about librarianship, and which of its aspects do you want to carry over into a new career?

Identify which of these factors is most important to you, and be honest about those on which you may be willing to compromise. Think also about what you are *not* looking for. What aspects of your current career do you want to be sure to avoid in your new one? What types of work do you find enervating and uninspiring? Jumping into a new career that duplicates the worst facets of your current position does you no good. Is it important to you to, say, avoid bureaucracy? To avoid low pay, micromanagement, inflexibility, or profits over people? Think about where you are willing to compromise and what tradeoffs you are willing to make. Would you sacrifice salary for flexibility? Independence for benefits? Geography for job satisfaction? Taking the time to establish both what you are looking for and what you are unwilling to accept will help point you toward a suitable path.

Like Stephanie Gerding (see sidebar on page 10), think about creating a personal "mission statement" to guide not only your choice of work, but how you conduct yourself throughout your career. A mission statement succinctly outlines your own priorities, and helps you keep focused on these in a constantly shifting environment. While you may choose to pursue a variety of careers

On a Mission

I entered the profession when technology was first becoming mainstream. I've always been interested in information transfer and learning, and have been able to combine my interests in writing, training, and technology into a career that I am passionate about—one that supports the important work of libraries.

I've never worked as a traditional librarian, but have held several very different library-related jobs, many that required an MLS. Each also required technology and training skills. I have worked for SIRSI as a library automation trainer, for Federal Express as a systems administrator and library manager, for the Bill & Melinda Gates Foundation doing technology installations and training, and for two state libraries, managing their continuing education statewide programs. Now I work from home, combining consulting activities such as providing workshops for libraries in Arizona and for other states, facilitation of meetings and events, and writing articles, books, a resource blog, and technical information. Typical daily tasks include networking, creating handouts and curriculum, writing, face-to-face and online training, facilitating, online learning, and project planning.

I love working from home! I am also grateful to be able to use the skills I have to best serve the library profession. I believe in libraries and want to support them, and my alternative career lets me do that. (I also appreciate less time spent in meetings!)

The one thing I learned in library school that stands out as most useful is not specifically library related. As a course assignment in a library management class taught by the acting dean, Dr. David Penniman, we were asked to write a personal mission statement that described what would guide our actions. I still live by that same mission, and refer to it at least once a year to see if I'm on track. I really believe that course and Dr. Penniman taught me a lot about taking risks and about making decisions based on a long-range strategy. It helped me make the leap to working for myself, since I realized it was the best use of my skills and abilities, and is what I love to do.

I have also found that it is very important to make personal connections with people. Join committees; ask people to have lunch; go to library gatherings. Don't ever be afraid to ask for advice from someone you admire or who is doing work you'd like to be involved with. Most people will be flattered to share their experience. Also, always ask to be paid for your work. Many librarians undervalue themselves. It never hurts to ask. If you don't ask to be paid, guess what—you won't be! There isn't anything wrong with doing *some* volunteer work, but the library field is very different from the business world in that respect.

Librarians are very well suited to alternative careers, and I know of many young professionals who are able to explore many different options while staying under the umbrella of librarianship. I am grateful to have entered a profession that has allowed me to pursue many different avenues.

Stephanie Gerding is an independent library consultant and author, Phoenix, AZ.

throughout your life, having a sense of your core mission and values helps you stay true to yourself and find an underlying theme through whatever combination of careers you pursue.

Assessing Strengths

Once you have a general picture of what you want in your career, think about the skills, talents, and knowledge you already possess that can help you get to that point. Finding new ways to use and develop the skills you have acquired as an information professional (as well as those you've picked up through previous careers, education, or interests) is essential from the moment you begin to contemplate an alternative path. Skills and strengths that may be tangential or even unused in your current job may grow to become integral to your new career; those that you think of only in the library context can be reframed and used in other contexts. This can sometimes be as simple as changing the language you use to describe what you do.

In the discussions about transferable skills in later chapters, you will find that specific sets of useful skills, personality traits, talents, and knowledge bases will differ depending on your preferred career path. From the outset, though, look at the skills you've developed throughout your library career with fresh eyes. Even if you don't yet have a particular path in mind, you can use your research knowledge and the resources available at your current institution or school to identify possible career paths, determine what skills and education you might need, learn the fundamentals of starting your own business, or build the contacts and knowledge you need to strike out on your own.

Begin identifying your relevant skills by broadening your job search. Take some time to browse current ads for jobs in the fields you are considering, and make note of the desired skills listed by potential employers. How do these match up with your existing skills? How can you make the argument that your library knowledge and duties transfer? What can you do to fill in any gaps? Think broadly here. Many of the skills we learn as librarians are widely transferable, whether we've been managers, foreign language catalogers, or reference librarians. We tend to think of library work as something unique, when actually it utilizes many of the same skills and strengths needed in other fields.

Take some time to assess your personal strengths and weaknesses. Think about the times when you have had the opportunity to shine in your current (or previous) career, and times when you have been stifled. Think about areas where you excel, which may or may not be typical "librarian" areas. For example, are you good at one or more of the following? What else might you add to this list?

- Ability to handle change
- Analysis
- Attention to detail
- Being in charge
- Budgeting
- Building networks
- Communication
- Customer service
- Decision making
- Fixing computers
- Fundraising
- Handling stress
- Innovation
- Leadership
- Learning new things
- Marketing
- Organization
- Problem solving

- Public speaking

- Relationship building

- Researching

- Training

- Writing

These skills can carry over and help determine your new career path. Write down all of your own major skills and strengths, whether or not they're listed here. Try to prioritize them. Where are you strongest? What strengths and skills would you most like to use in a new career?

Realize that any list includes both hard skills (fixing computers) and personal strengths or traits (attention to detail). Make an honest assessment of your weaknesses as well; this isn't a job interview, so you can be frank with yourself. If you understand where you are not as strong, you can either shore up those skills or avoid choosing a career that requires strengths you lack.

Assessing your strengths and redefining them outside of the narrow box of "librarianship" also helps you broaden your horizons. As G. Kim Dority, author of *Rethinking Information Work*, stresses:

> If we reframe our skill set from "librarianship" to the larger and more encompassing "information work," then we have choices that can respond to changes in job markets, personal financial requirements, living arrangements, and other professional and life circumstances. We may be information professionals who choose to spend our entire careers in the library field, in traditional libraries. But if budgets continue to be cut, staffs continue to be downsized, and jobs become scarce in times of economic crisis, information professionals can *always* deploy their skill sets in new directions

should they need or want to. ... The more broadly you consider your career and your professional skills, the more numerous—and rewarding—your career opportunities.[4]

Think about your skills in broader terms than "library work" generally allows; this helps you to explore broader options.

Not only will you need to identify your skills, you will also need to think about reframing these in terms the people in your new career path will understand. Instead of thinking like a librarian, you'll need to adopt a different mindset and think like a CEO, or a vendor, or an editor, using language that resonates in their environment. This can be as simple as changing the words you use to describe what you can do, or as complex as defining entirely new ways you can use your skills. Move away from library jargon. Think of your duties, long-term projects, and day-to-day tasks in terms of their component parts. For instance, do you work with the public? You may have picked up skills in communication, customer service, dealing with difficult people, marketing, and training. Rather than just listing specific job tasks, talk about what you have done in terms of the skills employers value in the career you are targeting. (Find more on reframing your skills in Appendix A.)

Take some time also to identify the environments in which you function most effectively. Do you work well alone? On a team? In a structured environment? When passionate about your work? When challenged by your work? When managed closely? When given autonomy? This process, again, will help you narrow down possible fields and eliminate occupations that fail to match your strengths.

You may simply ask yourself a series of questions aimed at getting to the heart of who you are and where you fit, or you may choose to undertake a more formal personality or career assessment using tools such as Myers-Briggs, Keirsey, Enneagram, or the

Strong Interest Inventory. If you are currently in school, your career center or guidance office may offer one or more of these formal assessments; if not, you can take online assessments or visit an assessment center or career counselor. (Find a number of links to online tools at www.quintcareers.com/career_assessment.html; find more on self-assessment for info pros in G. Kim Dority's *Rethinking Information Work.*)

Making Plans

Goal setting will be discussed in later chapters in terms of individual career paths, but any well thought-out career plan requires an honest assessment of your personal goals. Factors to consider when planning for your career change include:

- Your timeline for making your move
- Your financial requirements
- Ways to incorporate your strengths and values
- Where you picture yourself in one year, in five years

Having a clear set of goals, even if these change over time, keeps you focused. Visualize your ideal workday in your new career. What does it look like? Where are you? Who are you with? What are you doing? Is it a large company or small? Are you working alone or on a team? Is your organization for profit or nonprofit?

Your goals can also include components that fit into or alongside of your career path. Is one of your career goals to write a book? This can either turn into another career or exist comfortably alongside your library career. Do you want to go back to school to earn a second master's degree, finish your BA, or simply gain additional education? Think about what additional goals this might feed into: Will a degree help you launch a business, get a promotion, or get a better job in another field?

Taking the time to plan your new career also prevents you from rushing into a bad fit in your haste to escape your old job. Be sure that you are moving toward something, not just running away from your current position. Rather than chasing a career because you hear it will soon be "hot," or that there will be plenty of opportunity for people like you, take the time to find the best match for your own strengths and priorities.

Arguing Your Case

Although people in your personal network can be integral in making the leap, well-meaning friends, relatives, and colleagues may react to your new career plans with thinly disguised horror, especially if you currently have a "good" job, have spent your hard-earned time and money on an MLS, or are moving to a field for which they have less inherent respect. Your choice to change seems to somehow threaten their own decisions and outlook. It will be easier to counter their arguments if you are passionate about your new work, and if you have a firm plan rather than a vague idea of doing "anything but libraries." Realize that others' definitions of success may differ from yours; you need to find your own definition and stick to your guns.

Former colleagues or new library acquaintances might also project their own values onto your choices, accusing you of abandoning the field or selling out. This reflects less on you than on their own insecurities; the urge to belittle someone for making different choices reveals an underlying concern that one's own choices aren't good enough. Ignore them. Find more on this in Chapter 11, Where To from Here?, but suffice it to say here that you will need to be prepared for this type of reaction.

When your family depends on your income—or even when you alone depend on your income—the idea of moving into a new and possibly less stable career can be terrifying. Especially if you are striking out on your own, you must also consider how to replace the benefits of your current job. Consider practicalities like: Are you vested in a state retirement plan? Should you leave the money in or take it out? What will you do about health insurance if you decide to pursue freelance or part-time work? (More on this in Chapter 5, Building a Business.) Think ahead here—if you move into a new career now, you may have to start at the bottom and work your way back up, but you may have much higher long-term earning and promotion potential later in your career.

Building a Support System

Your personal network can be invaluable when making the decision about where to go next. Who knows you better than your friends, your work colleagues, your family? Choose one or more people to use as a sounding board as you work through outlining your values and your goals; ask for advice and for referrals to others who might be able to help. Other people sometimes have a better handle on your strengths and abilities, because they see you from the outside and can be somewhat more impartial. They can help you maintain perspective, and, because your closest support system most likely shares similar values, they can help keep you grounded. Ask them if they can envision you working in the field(s) you are considering. Ask what you may be missing. Ask for help with your resume and identifying transferable skills.

In any nontraditional career, your network of library (and nonlibrary) contacts will prove invaluable. Particularly if you decide to embark on a freelance career, set up a consulting company, start a research business, or provide workshops for libraries or librarians, your first few gigs will likely come from people you already know—and who already know you and your abilities. If you are seeking a new career, you are statistically most likely to find a job lead from someone you know. Let your whole network of colleagues know that you are starting this new career, and outline the types of work for which you are available. Stay involved in relevant professional associations; volunteer to present at professional events, and otherwise get the word out there about your services.

Your network of contacts outside of libraries comes into play when you seek a new position outside of traditional librarianship. If you have your heart set on a career in publishing and have previously published in the library field, you already have relationships with editors, who you can tap for advice. If you are interested in working for a vendor, strike up conversations with everyone manning a booth in the exhibit hall at your next library conference, and chat with the vendors' representatives you deal with at your current library. Get to know people in your chosen field, and build a support system of people committed to your success, from family and friends to mentors and ex-coworkers.

Those who have moved to nontraditional positions emphasize the importance of strong networks, one saying: "Networking was a huge influence on my career path—most of the positions that I've gained, library and otherwise, have been invited. Consequently, my personal/professional network has been very important in pursuing a nontraditional path." Pay it forward by helping others as well.

Think also about using technology to build on and take advantage of your network. Sites such as LinkedIn (www.linkedin.com) can be useful in keeping track of your professional network and drawing on extended connections. Recruiters now troll LinkedIn and similar sites for potential candidates, especially in technology-related fields, so keeping up your profile on these types of social networks can serve multiple purposes.

Building Balance

Many of those surveyed for this book expressed a desire to build more balance into their lives, whether this involved working from home, finding a career that allowed for more flexible hours, moving to part-time or freelance work, or choosing a career path that simply consumed less time and energy.

If you are considering leaving your library job primarily for personal or family reasons, be sure to think over your decision carefully. Are there ways to build better balance into your current job so that it better meets your and your family's current needs? In our female-dominated profession, we tend not always to advocate for our own best interests, assuming that "it is what it is" and that organizational policies and procedures are fixed and unchangeable. If you are seeking better balance, what might create this in your existing career? Partial telecommuting? Job sharing? Flexible hours? While these benefits may very well be negotiable, your employer is not going to go out of its way to offer them to you—you have to ask. Present a well thought-out plan to your administration, and see what happens. If they say no, you are no worse off than before, and you can then go on to find a new job or strike out on your own. If you are seeking better compensation, again, think about how to negotiate a raise and possibly a promotion. Have you been taking on additional duties? Has your job expanded beyond its original scope? Have you initiated successful new programs and services or won grants for your institution? Is there an upper-level position opening up for which you are well suited? The ability to argue for what you are worth is important, whether you choose to remain in your library or move on to other options.

Optimally, find ways to move around roadblocks rather than removing yourself from the workforce entirely. As Leslie Bennetts notes: "... there are frustrations and obstacles in any career, and when men hit roadblocks, they figure out ways to get around them. For women, however, having children provides the perfect excuse to give up. When full-time mothers discuss their own work histories in greater depth, frustration and disillusionment emerge again and again. Instead of finding more meaningful work, or more flexible work, or figuring out new strategies to overcome barriers, they decided to exit the arena entirely."[5]

Consider the long-term implications of leaving paid work, and explore all of your options. Even if, for example, your current salary covers little more than childcare and work-related costs, understand that being out of the workforce for a number of years has a long-term impact on your earning and promotion potential. Think about alternatives like exploring work with a family-friendly company, such as those on *Working Mother* magazine's annual "100 Best Companies" list (www.workingmother.com/web?service= vpage/109). Research other award-winning employers at Catalyst (www.catalyst.org) and on *Fortune* magazine's annual list of the best companies to work for (money.cnn.com/magazines/fortune/ bestcompanies/2007). If you choose to move to part-time or freelance employment, think about ways to keep up your library connections, knowledge, and skills. (See more on this in Chapter 10, Back Into the Fold.)

Again, decide on your own priorities here. If you wish to avoid putting your children in daycare, consider what kinds of careers lend themselves to flexibility, telecommuting, or odd hours where you can trade off childcare with a partner. If you wish to avoid a long commute, what kinds of careers might allow you to work from or near home?

Assessing Your Options

Once you've gone through this reflection and analysis, you will have a better idea of where your strengths lie and in what direction you might wish to take your talents. Once you have determined your direction, you can then turn your attention to marketing your transferable skills to potential employers. As one survey respondent explains: "Just jump in and try it! Most of my career

Missing the Coffee

My first job out of library school was as a children's librarian at a large public library in Colorado. This worked up until my son was born; I'm a single mom, and it was incredibly difficult for me to find childcare for mandatory night/weekend hours. My supervisor was not inclined to be flexible or even sympathetic. So, I moved back to the DC area to be near family and lucked into a job with DC Public Library (DCPL)—which not only paid better, but also had 9-to-5 hours.

Still, I wasn't too happy about spending such long hours away from my son (DC traffic made for a rough commute), so I searched for an even better solution. I found a job as a school librarian at a private school, one my son would be able to attend when he turned three. Unfortunately, the job was eliminated after a year due to lack of funding—so much for that plan! I found another private school job, but had some serious disagreements with administration about the role of a librarian.

This job finally drove me to explore alternate career paths. I set up my own Web site, advertised my services on craigslist as a freelance researcher, and landed a few big jobs. Suddenly it was all (more or less!) working; I was officially making it as a freelancer. I get to have my son with me 24/7, which I love, although it makes work challenging at times.

I'm always working on multiple projects. Right now, I'm fact checking for a publishing house, working as a contributing author to an upcoming nonfiction book on world religions (I do more writing than researching most days), and working as a Web content editor. I also do a little after-school tutoring, so my son and I can get out of the house once in a while. You need to diversify; you can't market just one skill, especially initially.

Research is my selling point; tutoring definitely grew out of being a children's/school librarian, an all-around homework helper and resource person. Life these days is kind of like library school all over again (only with a small child this time)—lots of research, lots of writing, lots of deadlines. I did need to learn a bit about marketing, which I was involved in a bit at DCPL. And, I needed to learn about logistics and time management, skills I had acquired as a single mom.

I love that I get positive feedback all the time, and that the more I work, the more I earn. I do not love the fact that I really do work 7 days a week, all day, every day. When I always have some deadline looming, it's hard to take a break. (But then, it's better than having no deadlines, as that would mean no work!)

I do miss the job security. I miss having someone else make the coffee. I miss leftover goodies in the break room. But, I do not miss having to leave my son in daycare all day. I'd rather miss coffee and cookies and a pension than miss him.

Maria Scinto is the Virtual Librarian, www.yourvirtual librarian.com, Washington, DC.

path was pure happenstance. I sold myself first on why I should take a certain job and then made sure I sold the prospective employer. Hard to believe, but you know in your gut whether or not it will be right for you." Find ideas and inspiration throughout this book as you consider possibilities for your own career. Realize, though, that the information provided here is not sufficient to make you into an information broker, a vendor, or a prospect researcher—the following chapters simply give some ideas on paths you might choose, how your skills might transfer, and how you might begin making the transition.

Chapters 2 and 3 talk about shifting your path just slightly by transferring your skills to organizations that either serve or resemble libraries. Your library skills transfer most easily and obviously to these types of environments, so use these possibilities as a jumping-off point for your own alternative career.

Endnotes

1. Barbara Sher, *Refuse to Choose! A Revolutionary Program for Doing Everything That You Love,* New York: Rodale, 2006: 53.

2. For these statistics and other information on the current employment status of new grads, see Stephanie Maatta, "Starting Pay Breaks $40K— Placements & Salaries 2005," *Library Journal* Oct. 15, 2006, www.libraryjournal.com/article/CA6379540.html (accessed Oct. 4, 2007), and Stephanie Maatta, What's an MLIS Worth?" *Library Journal* Oct. 15, 2007, www.libraryjournal.com/article/CA6490671.html (accessed Oct. 16, 2007).

3. Julie Jansen, *I Don't Know What I Want, But I Know It's Not This: A Step-by-Step Guide to Finding Gratifying Work,* New York: Penguin, 2003: 10.

4. G. Kim Dority, *Rethinking Information Work: A Career Guide for Librarians and Other Information Professionals,* Westport, CT: Libraries Unlimited, 2006: 2–3.

5. Leslie Bennetts, *The Feminine Mistake: Are We Giving Up Too Much?* New York: Hyperion, 2007: 45.

Chapter 2

Organizations Serving Libraries and Librarians

Engaging in a single career or lifelong trade is no longer the way we work or will work in the future. Instead, the demands of the marketplace as well as our personal lifestyle choices dictate the kind of work we do and the way we structure it. Because of this, the capacity to shift gears more easily where work is concerned has become a critical skill for those intent on achieving a significant measure of life satisfaction.[1]

One way to move into an alternative career while still remaining close to your librarian roots is to explore options with the organizations and companies that serve librarians and libraries. Who better to understand libraries' needs than someone with personal experience in the field? Vendors and other library-related organizations often advertise on library job boards, recruit at library conferences, use library staffing firms to locate candidates, or otherwise specifically seek out employees with library backgrounds. Library and information science (LIS) schools and library technical assistant (LTA) programs specifically seek MLS-degreed librarians, especially to teach as part-time adjunct professors. Library associations, state libraries, and systems benefit from staff with working library experience. When moving to an organization somehow connected to libraries, it can be easier to see how your library skills transfer.

To learn what kinds of skills and background might be useful in these types of related organizations, consider going on informational interviews. Visit someone who is currently working in your target field; ask them questions about their particular job, their company, the industry as a whole, and the skills and knowledge that have made them successful. You can also think about offering your services to one of these organizations on a volunteer or intern basis to gain some experience, although this may be more difficult to arrange if you aren't currently in school.

Vendors

Vendors recognize that many of their best employees come from the library world, paving the way for you to make your case. Check out the exhibits at ALA Annual or any other large library conference to get an idea of the range and types of vendors out there. Use conference lists of participating vendors or the listings at the Librarian's Yellow Pages Online (librariansyellowpages.com) to identify potential employers. Talk to the salespeople and trainers who call or visit your own library; find out how they first got into the field and ask for their insights and advice. Organize and participate in conference panels that include vendor representatives to help build your network.

Identify your own strengths in terms of the skills in demand by various vendors: Are you a top-notch programmer? Do you have excellent people skills? Do you enjoy marketing your current institution to its clientele? Can you catalog, classify, and organize with the best of them? Some directly transferable skills and experience to positions with vendors include:

- Abstracting
- Cataloging
- Collection development

- Customer service

- Indexing

- Marketing

- Organization of knowledge

- People skills

- Reference

- Technology knowledge

- Training ability

Careers with vendors include, but are not limited to, working for an integrated library system (ILS) or database vendor doing sales, tech support, or training; contracting out as a virtual reference worker with a company like QuestionPoint; indexing, abstracting, or creating and maintaining thesauri or taxonomies for database vendors; cataloging for jobbers; and working as a staffer for a library temp or employment agency. Look for ads for jobs in areas such as sales, virtual reference, and technical support, or for job titles such as account representative, account manager, trainer, bibliographer, or cataloger. Think about how your library experience best translates into the vendor environment. If you have collection development or technical services experience, maybe a jobber is right for you. If you have been a systems librarian, maybe an ILS or database vendor could be the place. If you have marketing experience, you might target sales or account representative positions. If you have worked with serials or electronic resources, you might fit in well with a subscription agent or database vendor. If you have worked with the public and trained them on library databases, you might be able to provide similar training to librarians, or weigh in on user-centered design. Don't limit yourself to positions that exactly match your previous experience, but do realize how far this experience extends and where it allows you to market yourself most easily.

A job with a vendor can also be a good choice for new grads who find during library school that they are drawn to some areas of information work but not to others; working for vendors allows them to avoid the less personally appealing aspects of traditional libraries. Alexander Feng, Technical Content Coordinator, SirsiDynix, Huntsville, AL, explains: "I realized that I enjoyed certain aspects of libraries (information organization, retrieval, gathering), but not so much other aspects (weeding, collection development). Looking at the library landscape vis-à-vis the Internet, I realized that, for me, a traditional library setting was not what I wanted, but something that melded the forefront of the Internet with the wonderful landscape of knowledge and knowledge services that libraries provide. This brought me to a library services vendor, where I am helping develop tools for libraries, bridging the print world of libraries with the increasingly digital landscape."

Ready for Change

After 33+ years working in academic and public library settings, I was ready for a new challenge. I never expected to find myself interested in working as a sales rep for a vendor to libraries, but I had some very good sales reps call on me while working as a librarian, and I learned a lot from them and reframed my view of the sales world.

As regional account manager, I generate new business for my employer. I make several in-person sales calls to noncustomers and current customers each month, respond to needs from current customers, and represent my company at state, regional, and national library conferences. I must be able to respond intelligently to questions, be articulate and skillful in gleaning information from prospective customers, and offer them solutions to their current problems.

The best thing about my career is the challenge—I am learning new things every day, developing my skills, and enjoying the stimulation and variety. I like least the sense of isolation from coworkers, and I do miss the one-on-one reference/helping interview and the friendships that develop in the workplace. I don't, however, miss the 40-hour routine at the library!

With my experience and knowledge, I feel more confidence in understanding the needs and situations of librarians, and I am better able to offer them solutions that benefit them. I use my library background and education daily in working with my company and with customers, but I needed to acquire experience with sales techniques, formulating the right questions, listening better, finesse, and manners.

Anyone following a similar path should be open to risk-taking. Talk to people who are in a similar alternative career and find out what they like and dislike about it; ask your new employer for what you need; re-evaluate your needs as you enter the new nontraditional job; learn negotiation skills; remember to be patient; don't expect to ever stop learning (or making mistakes!). Realize that no transition is going to be perfect, and the flaws, drawbacks, challenges, and bumps turn out to be one's best teachers. Don't obsess about preparing for the change, but be aware of your strengths and weaknesses and the kinds of situations in which you work best. Also, be open to finding out lots of new things about yourself as you transition. What fun and surprises await you!

Paul Duckworth is Regional Account Manager, BWI (Book Wholesalers, Inc.), Lexington, KY.

Many of those who have made the move to the "dark side" and now work for a vendor appreciate having the opportunity to work with multiple libraries, recognizing the broad range of experiences and understanding of the field this provides. As Sophia Apostol, Information Services Librarian, Seneca College, Toronto, Ontario, explains about her former sales manager position with YBP Library Services: "Working with customers is the fun part of the job. Interacting with different librarians and library staff from many institutions gives you such a breadth of knowledge about libraries in general."

A library background is tremendously helpful to any position with a library vendor. Librarians know how the decision-making process in libraries works, know what libraries need, understand librarians' real-world frustrations, and speak their language. Apostol continues: "So many skills are transferable! Training librarians to use a new system is analogous to instructing students on how to use journal indexes. Answering customer questions is like working the reference desk and providing virtual reference. In both careers there are many, many meetings and projects to be juggled and priorities to be set. Committee work is always present in both careers. Having been trained as a librarian was extremely useful for me when working for a vendor because I was able to speak to librarians in our own language, and more fully understand the issues and challenges faced in libraries."

Realize that many positions with vendors, especially in sales, training, or support, will require quite a bit of travel, either to visit customer sites or to represent the company at library-related conferences and meetings. If you are less comfortable with the idea of frequent travel or have family commitments that preclude your absence, you might investigate other options. Vendor work, even when it resembles library work, can also be at least as stressful (if not more so!) than library work. Jonathan Boyne, Chat Reference Librarian, QuestionPoint 24/7 Reference, suggests: "Don't [do it] unless you can take high stress. Like being counter help at McDonald's at rush hour, but many expect Cordon Bleu and think they're the only patron you're helping."

Library vendors often advertise on niche online job boards, so you can familiarize yourself with the types of positions available by browsing the ads at LISjobs.com and other library-related job banks. If you are seeking a particular type of job, such as cataloger, be sure to join relevant email discussion lists like AUTOCAT (listserv. syr.edu/archives/autocat.html). Identify the major vendors who hire for the types of positions you are targeting and bookmark their individual human resources sites. Vendors frequently seek MLS librarians, LTAs, or employees with library experience who understand the unique library market, so don't skip over these ads on the assumption that you fail to qualify. Some sample verbiage from vendor job ads posted online during summer 2007 follows:

- Position Requirements: Bachelor's Degree, MLS preferred. Demonstrated sales ability in the book/journal trade. Excellent communication skills. Exceptional organizational skills. Negotiation skills. Above average computer skills (Excel, Word, Outlook, CRM, PowerPoint, Internet). Ability to travel 65% of the time.

- Do you love libraries? Then you may want to explore the idea of working with us ... an international bookseller with a history of quality, stability and growth has an immediate opening for a Bibliographic and Technical Services Account Manager ... We are looking for a motivated individual with academic library technical experience, an MLS degree, and exceptional customer service skills.

- A minimum of 3 years experience in Library, Publishing or a related field preferred. Bachelor's degree (B.A.) from a four-year college or university and one to two years related

experience and/or training or equivalent preferred. Must
be able to speak, read and write Spanish and English.

Just as when applying for jobs in libraries, if you have *most* of the
skills advertised, apply anyway—then use your cover letter and
resume to make the case as to how your specific skills and experience make up for any requirements you lack. For example, if a company is looking for "demonstrated sales ability," you can talk about
your knowledge of the library market and of what librarians are
looking for. You can talk about how you have marketed library services to patrons and increased circulation, attendance at programs,
or any other measurable statistics. You can talk about how you led
a push for a successful referendum, or convinced a municipal
board to increase your library's budget, or any other example of
how you have "sold" your institution to its community. (Find more
on retooling your resume and making your case in Appendix A.)

Non-MLS library workers are often able to find better opportunities with vendors, who aren't hung up on the primacy of the
degree, than they can in traditional libraries. Many vendors are
open to hiring and promoting non-MLS staff with a library background. If you have been working in libraries for some time, yet
have little opportunity for promotion because you lack an MLS,
think about bringing that experience to a related field that is less
focused on the specific degree. Some vendors may even pay for
you to earn your MLS or for other education if it would be helpful
in your new career; most are very good about providing on-the-job
training, giving you a chance to acquire any specific skills and
competencies you need before diving into your new position.

Many library vendors hire for positions that translate almost
directly into their library equivalents, using the same skill set, education, and expertise. BWI, Follett, Baker & Taylor, and other jobbers, for instance, often post openings for catalogers and copy
catalogers, who perform very similar tasks to library catalogers, but
in a corporate environment. EBSCO and other database vendors

hire indexers, abstractors, and taxonomists. If you enjoy your work as a librarian or library paraprofessional, but dislike your particular working environment, this type of move might be the answer. Heather McDonough, Proprietary Database Editor, EBSCO Publishing, Ipswich, MA, explains: "Our ultimate goal is the same as the goal of librarians: to provide the best-quality research tool possible to library patrons. A lot of the positions I have personally held have incorporated skills related to librarianship, including writing abstracts; indexing using an LCSH-based set of headings; creating subject-specific thesauri; understanding computers, applications, and other technology; performing research, editing and quality control tasks; managing people; etc."

Be aware that the jump to the corporate world will require a different way of looking at things. You'll need, for instance, to adjust to a for-profit mentality—and to the notion that people may actually get fired! Some librarians may accuse you of abandoning the profession, or turning to the "dark side," defining you by something as simple as the vendor affiliation on your nametag at conferences, and assuming in every conversation that you have an underlying agenda. Those who have had negative experiences with a vendor or who are passionately committed to libraries and librarianship may see you as a sellout, so be prepared for negative reactions from some of your colleagues—and be ready to do what is best for you.

Advantages to vendor work can include better pay, more variety, the opportunity to travel, the chance to work with multiple libraries and build far-flung networks, new challenges, better professional development opportunities, being on the cutting edge of technology, and the chance to do something different. Consider how these possibilities match up with what you are looking for in an alternative career. With some vendors, you might also have the opportunity to telecommute either full- or part-time, especially if you accept a sales position covering a region away from the vendor's home office; but you may need to get comfortable with managing

Creating Connections

I was an attorney for seven years before becoming a law librarian at the New Jersey branch office of a large New York-based law firm. I held that job for three years (without an MLIS) before joining Thomson West as a Librarian Relations Manager, and obtained my MLIS while employed by Thomson West. I became a Librarian Relations Manager because I was tired of sitting at a desk eight hours/day, five days/week. I love to teach and lecture, so the Librarian Relations Manager position let me combine my legal background, my love of computers/research and my love of teaching/lecturing into one job! After almost four years in that position, I became a Manager of New Product Development for Thomson West. This new position allows me to create new and innovative products for West's customers while making the most of my various work-related perspectives in the process—attorney, customer, librarian, trainer/educator.

As a Librarian Relations Manager, I was the connection between the large law firm librarians in New Jersey, Pennsylvania, and Delaware and Thomson West. I offered training sessions, both on-site and in large-group settings. I provided customer service in terms of taking the librarians' concerns/suggestions back to the right people at West. I helped fund local professional association events. I spoke at local library schools. I chaired, presented, and/or sponsored presentations at the national law librarian association meetings. I wrote articles for law librarian publications. Over the past year, I used my medical malpractice background to help some of our product developers develop and release a medical/legal research project. It was this experience that led me to my new position in New Product Development. I found the experience of taking a product from an idea in someone's head to a product that helps West's customers maximize and improve their research experience absolutely fascinating. So, when offered the chance to work from the headquarters office on exciting new projects, I couldn't refuse!

Before I got the MLIS, I knew *what* law librarians did on a daily basis. Now, I understand the *why* behind it. I also can truly hold myself out as a peer to our librarian customers, as someone who understands what they are going through, since I worked in the field and obtained the education. Understanding human information behavior and computer usability issues, thanks to courses I took toward my MLIS, helps me work with people at West to make our products better for our customers, especially the law librarians.

My nonlibrary background has also been tremendously helpful in both my positions at West. In part, it's helped me better understand the products I use to teach to my customers. It also allowed me to help the product developers on this new medical/legal product, and sometimes helped me explain attorneys' behaviors to my law librarians who had not practiced law or gone to law school. In my new position, it gives me an additional perspective to bring to the job.

If you are interested in a librarian relations-type position, you really have to love to get up and speak in front of a group. Great presentation skills are a must! You also have to be a real self-starter. No one told me what to do on a daily basis— I just knew what needed doing, and made sure it got done. You have to want to build positive relationships with people, which can sometimes take a lot of hard work and perseverance. I do wish I'd known just how addicting my BlackBerry was going to be! It was very easy in the job to fall into the habit of never putting the work down. If you're not careful to set limits, you could easily work upward of 20 hours/day. That's not because anyone expects the Librarian Relations Managers to actually put in those kinds of hours; it's simply because they're driven to provide the best possible service and create/maintain the best possible relationships with their customers and co-workers.

As a Librarian Relations Manager, my job was to make the everyday life of my law librarian customers easier and better. My role allowed my customers to do their jobs well, stand out in their organizations, and educate their "patrons" (read: attorneys) on the terrific importance of the law librarian to any given law firm. I didn't have anywhere close to a 9-to-5 job. I enjoyed being able to work from home on occasion. I liked my customers and the opportunity to educate them and help them in their relationship with West. I didn't always enjoy being the only Librarian Relations Manager in my territory. It got lonely having no one to share ideas with on a daily basis. I missed actually doing [the kind of] research that I did as a law librarian the most. I loved answering questions and always got a kick out of how much the attorneys appreciated what I did, even if the information was very easy for me to find. I didn't miss sitting at a desk all day long, every day ... at all!

Stephanie Fox is Manager, New Product Development, Thomson West, Eagan, MN.

people and/or building relationships over a distance—and learning to time your work to catch people across multiple time zones!

Vendors inherently have more money, and more flexibility with their money, than most libraries, and tend to put some of that money back into their staff. You might find that you have more opportunities to attend conferences and better access to continuing education and training. If professional development is important to you, look for work with a vendor who supports this. As Julie Harwell, Training Resources Manager, EBSCO Industries, writes: "One atypical benefit of working at EBSCO compared to a traditional library setting is how supportive the company is of our continued professional development. We are actively encouraged to attend and contribute to conferences and given adequate support to meet our professional goals. We don't have to vie with one another to attend conferences, nor do we have to share a room with five people just to be able to attend."[2]

Associations

Librarians often complain that their associations, especially the larger and more bureaucratic associations, fail to represent their interests effectively. One way to ensure that these groups remain both faithful to the principles of librarianship and relevant to library workers' current concerns is for librarians themselves to work at all levels of the organization. (See more on work with non-library associations in Chapter 7, Working in Very Different Roles).

Just as with vendor work, be aware that association work will likely require significant travel to conferences and other venues. Also be aware that as a staff person for an association, your words will be taken as representative of that association. This is a particular consideration for bloggers, whose personal blogs might be mistaken for mouthpieces of the organization.

You won't necessarily receive better monetary compensation with association work, but its fringe benefits include the chance to travel to association conferences and other events, to stay intimately involved with the profession, and to build networks with librarians across the region, country, or world. Another big plus is

A Fruitful Merger

I think the majority of my career has been alternative. I didn't choose my career path; it chose me. Since 2003, my work as ALA-APA (American Library Association-Allied Professional Association) director has been the perfect merger of library skills and skills introduced in business school like entrepreneurship, services marketing, and accounting. At ALA-APA, I serve the profession, not just librarians, but everyone concerned. I know what people are talking about and am sensitive. This takes a blend of LIS education, my varied library experience, and b-school exposure.

As ALA-APA director, I encourage library workers who deserve higher salaries, promote services like toolkit and certification, create and update policies and procedures, edit the monthly newsletter, serve as board and committee liaison, answer questions about the annual salary survey, ask people to help spread the word about ALA-APA, seek donations and sponsorships, update the Web site, plan conference programs, research for the WAGE project, prepare for speaking engagements, and supervise one staff member

My work is a blessing to me. I like that it's helping people, the variety, the encouragement and support of those who believe in the ALA-APA, my committees, starting something new, the missions and services of the organization, the skills I'm developing and expanding, my colleagues at ALA and in the field, travel and speaking, and the responsibility. Every day is still new, and I keep learning.

I do dislike the unrealistic expectations of some, the lack of buy-in by some of those who know about and influence the association, the lack of awareness and funding to make more people aware, fundraising, and the sacrifices that come with being in an underfunded entity.

I'd suggest that anyone interested in a similar career path just do it. I had no idea what I was in for, but I'm so thankful. It's an incredible challenge, but I know why I'm doing this—and get to hear every so often that it makes a difference to someone. I do miss the people I served and the feeling that I got with direct service, but miss least the monotony and frustration that can set in when a culture is resistant to change.

Jenifer Grady is Director, ALA-APA: The Organization for the Advancement of Library Employees, Chicago, IL.

the chance to effect change on a larger scale than just within your single library's community. Carrie Russell, Copyright Specialist, ALA's Office for Information Technology Policy, Washington, DC, describes her job as "ensur[ing] that federal information policy reflects the values of librarians and the mission of libraries," and explains that "I choose this particular type of work because I wanted to work at a national level; I believe these issues are important to democracy."

View positions available with ALA on the association's Web site (https://cs.ala.org/jobs/viewjobs.cfm). Look for listings of positions with other library-related associations on their respective Web sites and on the general library job boards, as well as in association publications.

State Libraries, Local Systems, and Consortia

Since both state libraries and local systems/consortia serve the library community, they seek staff with library backgrounds and work experience. As with associations, you have the opportunity to make a broader impact on the profession and the larger community by influencing and serving a wide variety of libraries.

System Savvy

I was a mid-life career changer. My previous life experience as a management consultant and retail manager played a large part in my getting hired as a system consultant, even though I had very little library experience. With 20+ years experience in management, corporate environments, supervision, teaching, training, and project work, I pretty much had the background I needed to be successful. I worked in business, and so had a very "bottom line" approach to results that served me well. Experience managing a budget was very helpful, and my familiarity with corporate HR and personnel/supervisory issues was equally valuable, as I didn't need to learn all of that from scratch. My LIS education, though, gave me a strong understanding of the function, aspirations, and limitations of library service in contemporary America.

I firmly believe that system librarian work at the state level is best accomplished by mature, experienced (read: older) people who have a reservoir of life experiences upon which to draw. Consulting in general requires not just technical know-how, but people skills and organizational savvy, which are not generally found in young librarians fresh out of school.

As a library development consultant, I do a lot of facilitation work with library boards of trustees, especially around strategic (long-term) planning. I organize (and sometimes deliver) training to our member libraries on topics like collection planning, weeding, automation, and space and facility planning. I consult on legal, governance, and legislative issues, and member libraries often call with questions about budgets, state aid, grants, technology, building projects, programming, personnel issues, and patron support. About 90 percent of my time is spent supporting the 46 public libraries in our region. School and academic libraries already have technology and administrative support systems in place, and therefore have less need of our services.

I most appreciate the contact with a variety of libraries and library staff. Since we serve tiny rural libraries along with large urban systems, there's a lot of diversity to enjoy. The part I like least is sorting through complex budget and finance issues for our libraries. We have city, township, county, and district libraries in our system, each with a slightly different funding mechanism. Moreover, with many libraries, unique arrangements and accommodations have been made with municipal governments over the years, resulting in a politically charged and highly sensitive funding environment unique to the library in question. It gets very challenging!

While I don't deal with patrons and programs per se, the notion of service is central to my job, just as it is to other librarians. My job is to help libraries improve their services to their patrons and to provide the necessary support for them to accomplish that goal. So, ultimately, our goal is the same: to improve the end-user's library experience. I visit libraries often, so am able to maintain a strong personal network among librarians and library staff, and remain active in statewide and regional library associations.

Mickey Coalwell is Library Development Consultant, Northeast Kansas Library System, Lawrence, KS.

Multitype library systems offer a number of ways for you to focus your work: You can work with a specific type of library (school, academic, public); concentrate on marketing or grants or training; and work directly with member institutions or stay more behind the scenes. One challenge in a multitype system or consortium, however, is how best to meet the needs of all of your members. It can be tempting to focus your efforts on the types of libraries you are most familiar with or in which you have personally worked.

Systems, state libraries, and consortia most often advertise on local library job boards, seeking candidates with local knowledge and a background in the types of libraries served. For many of these positions, you'll need an MLS plus several years of experience, making them a better option for those changing careers than for new grads.

LIS Schools

Librarians have always engaged in activities like bibliographic instruction, and, more recently, in technology instruction and instructional design. Librarianship and teaching are inherently allied in their educational mission, and your skills in training either patrons or colleagues transfer well into teaching other groups—especially potential librarians. (While this section discusses teaching or working in an LIS school, also read about teaching courses not related to libraries in Chapter 3, Organizations Similar to Libraries.) Especially if you lack experience training in your own institution, you may want to try out teaching in some sense before pursuing this option. Offer to conduct workshops for your local system or at a professional conference; volunteer to do technology training at your local public library.

If you are interested in teaching in an LIS program, your options include teaching full-time in an SLIS (which may require going back to school to earn your PhD), as well as teaching part-time as an adjunct instructor and/or teaching in a community college LTA program. Most librarians lack a PhD, making tenure track positions out of reach. It is possible in some schools to teach as a full-time lecturer, but at a lower salary and without the chance of tenure; part-time adjunct positions are much more common. Here, the MLS or other master's will serve as the minimum degree, and schools will generally seek recent and extensive experience in the subject area you will be teaching.

Technology also opens up additional opportunities to teach in LIS programs. Universities seeking adjunct lecturers for online courses, for example, may be open to employing distant faculty, allowing you to teach even if you aren't in close proximity to a library school. Realize that these types of adjunct positions can eat up more time than you might expect, especially when you are teaching or developing a new course and creating a syllabus from scratch. Your first couple of semesters can require a significant investment of time and resources, but things will settle down as you become more familiar with the topics covered and have the basic resources outlined. Although you might assume that online courses require less time, the opposite seems to be true. Be aware of the true commitment needed, especially if you are adding teaching onto an existing full-time job.

So, what's the best way to break into teaching? Your network of contacts will be invaluable here. Know someone who already teaches an LIS class? Have you kept in touch with any of your former professors from grad school? Let them know that you're available to come in and speak to their class. Start as a guest lecturer, and test the waters. Also, keep an eye on general library job boards and the ALISE (Association for Library and Information Science Education) job board (www.alise.org/mc/page.do?sitePageId=555 88&orgId=ali) as well as on relevant email discussion lists like jESSE (web.utk.edu/~gwhitney/jesse.html).

While it can be difficult to cobble together a living from adjunct teaching positions, this type of work can be a nice supplement to a day job, or serve as a piece of a patchwork career. An adjunct position combines very well with a full-time library job, allowing you to remain grounded in the practical realities of the profession and transmit your current real-world experience to students. (Be careful, though, to blend experience with theory, and be sure to generalize your personal experience in one library so that it applies to the many potential futures of your students.) Your practical experience can be a fantastic asset when it comes to preparing students for the real world of working in libraries. Cindy Mediavilla, Lecturer, UCLA, Library Programs Consultant, California State Library, and freelance consultant/trainer, shares: "My duties as adjunct faculty are the same as any teacher: lesson preparation, lecture, read and grade papers, and submit grades. But I also do a lot of informal advising, as I'm one of the few people in the department who has actually worked in the public library world and still has lots of contacts in the field."

Adjunct jobs can also combine well with other nontraditional part-time or freelance work. If you are a librarian author, for example, you might use the knowledge you have acquired in planning and teaching your course to write a book that can be used as a textbook for your class. If you are a consultant, freelance indexer, or columnist, you might appreciate some semi-steady teaching work to help fill in the gaps and keep some income flowing when between other gigs.

Tenure track teaching positions often include requirements for conducting research and publishing in a specific area of expertise, as well as presenting at conferences, serving on university and association committees, and engaging in other professional and service activities. The idea of "publish or perish" might be old hat to academic librarians making the switch; others may need to familiarize themselves with research tools and techniques. Keeping up with developments in the field and staying professionally active should be second nature to any committed librarian, so these requirements should be less than onerous. Your practical work in the field can translate into the ability to teach practical courses, which MLS students generally welcome.

Practical experience can also often substitute for teaching experience when applying to teach in an LIS program. A spring 2007 ad for a part-time lecturer in a digital libraries course, for instance, asked for: "Minimum two years experience in planning, implementing, and evaluating library, archives, museum or cultural heritage institution digitization projects and initiatives, *or* teaching a course or workshop that covers these topics" [emphasis added]. An ad around the same time for an online lecturer in a school of library and information studies specified a minimum of an MLS degree along with "Experience with management of libraries and information agencies, including: service needs assessment, goal and objective setting, staffing, budgeting and evaluation of programs and services required."

Watch for this type of verbiage and be able to play up your own real-world experience. Emphasize the advantages it brings, as well as any teaching or training background you may have. Just as when applying for jobs in libraries, see how well you can match up your specific experience and skills with those sought by a given school.

If you see teaching in an LIS program as a long-term commitment, you can also think about going back for the PhD, as did Cindy Mediavilla: "To become a better teacher and to acquire the research skills to become a good consultant, I felt compelled to pursue a doctorate. I would not recommend this path for everyone, but for me it changed the way I analyze situations and problems, which has been helpful on assessment projects."

Earning your doctorate will likely also give you an opportunity to gain teaching experience as a teaching assistant or to serve as a graduate assistant to a professor in your program, giving you some of the academic background you may currently lack. Visit any LIS schools near you that offer doctoral programs; make an appointment to talk to an advisor, a professor, or the admissions office.

Doctoral Pursuits

Before earning my PhD and moving into my teaching position, I worked in libraries for almost 13 years. I had been pondering further education with the ultimate goal of a faculty position in an LIS school, but my situation made it impossible to pull up stakes and move to a town with an LIS PhD program. While working with the staff development team at my former workplace to evaluate how we developed future library leaders, I did some research into the ways library employees could earn their MLS, in Indiana or beyond. Online classes offered at the University of Illinois were intriguing, but were only for master's students.

I pondered the virtually impossible commute to Bloomington or Ann Arbor from South Bend. I also began fact-finding and soul-searching to make sure I was ready for such a big step if an opportunity appeared; IM and email conversations with library colleagues helped me decide I was ready for the challenge of doctoral pursuits. In 1994, I was very excited to receive an email with information about the University of North Texas (UNT) distance-independent PhD program. I applied and was accepted! I began my two years of coursework in June 2004, wrote my dissertation in 2006–2007, and graduated in August 2007.

In my current position, I do all of the professor-like things one might expect: I teach, advise students, attend faculty meetings, serve on university committees, write, and speak. Daily I might finalize a class lecture (and tweak a presentation), read a chapter or two of the students' required reading to refresh my memory, and devote time to writing, editing articles, and blogging. It all seems to feed into the next thing.

I love the interaction with students and the opportunity to help them learn about the profession. I love to lead discussions in class about issues we've read about. Everything I did in my public library job prepared me to teach in LIS. I had no idea then, but every meeting, every kerfuffle my library had with the public (Madonna's *SEX* book, etc.) now becomes useful in my work with students. I did have to learn the ins and outs of academia. I once asked a professor at UNT if we'd ever have a class on dealing with problem students, university politics, and what it means to be part of "the Academy." "Nope," she said, "you pick all that up on our own." I do miss being out on the edge—looking at ways to improve service with technology and ways to empower the staff to work better. But, I don't miss the meetings—I think every library job comes with too many meetings!

If someone is interested in pursuing the PhD and teaching in LIS, I would urge them to do so—to look for ways to make it happen. However, I honestly believe the best LIS educators are those who have worked in libraries, especially those with experience in various types of libraries. This library degree still is very practical, and practical experience paired with classroom know-how is perfect for the field.

Michael Stephens is Assistant Professor, Dominican University, River Forest, IL.

Keep an eye out for scholarship opportunities for doctoral candidates, especially if you intend to concentrate in an area like school media, public libraries, or technology. A concern about sufficient faculty to teach the "librarians of the future" has created a push to attract more working librarians—especially from outside of academia—to doctoral programs, creating additional opportunities. Programs like Emporia's offer of a combination of weekend and distance coursework to help accommodate working librarians pursuing their PhD (slim.emporia.edu/programs/programs.htm). Doctoral funding opportunities include the ALA Spectrum Doctoral Fellowship (www.ala.org/ala/diversity/spectrum/phd fellowship/phd.htm).

Those interested in teaching in an LIS program and/or earning a PhD should investigate ALISE (www.alise.org). ALISE membership benefits include a subscription to the *Journal of Education for Library and Information Science*, reduced conference fees, conference placement services, and a quarterly enewsletter; they also offer a reduced rate for students. The jESSE email discussion list (web.utk.edu/~gwhitney/jesse.html), devoted to discussion of library and information science education issues, includes position announcements and professional development opportunities for faculty—as well as often spirited discussions on all aspects of LIS education.

You can also think about pursuing nonteaching positions in LIS schools, where your library background or MLS will offer an obvious advantage in connecting with the students and understanding the ins and outs of the program.

A career with an LIS program can be seen as part of the broader world of information work, rather than an alternative career per se. As one survey respondent puts it: "My current profession is part of librarianship, since we train and educate future librarians. I see this as a nontraditional path within our broader field." What you learn by teaching adjunct also carries over to your day job, especially in an academic library, where your further immersion into the academy lends itself to increased credibility and respect. If you teach locally, you can get to know your students, grab up the cream of the crop as interns for your own library—and then hire them later! Teaching in an LIS program gives you the opportunity to mentor and connect with a new generation of librarians, and lets you remain a part of the larger profession. It also helps keep you fresh, current, and intellectually challenged—your students, not having yet inculcated the "way we've always done it," may ask provocative questions that make you think about larger professional issues in a fresh way.

Fortuitous Flexibility

I decided to pursue a library degree hoping it would allow me to have a challenging career that also offered some flexibility in the ever-elusive balance between work and family. After library school, I worked for a little more than two years in a variety of libraries—government, solo, and an independent, private library. My last library job, at the independent, member-driven library, had a small staff, so I looked forward to learning all the ins and outs of the institution. At the time, though, I also had an infant daughter, and the strict schedule demanded of a small staff meant that the very reason I went into the field—flexibility—was completely gone. On the day I came to this realization, I fortuitously ran into my former dean. He offered me a part-time job as the Webmaster for the Simmons GSLIS program, and my new career was born, eventually becoming full-time.

I work in both curriculum and communications. For curriculum, I schedule the program's courses, work with faculty to make decisions about the curriculum, and am part of the team that helps support the registration processes. Daily tasks include regular contact with adjunct and full-time faculty regarding their schedules, course requirements, and registration issues; working with faculty on committees dealing with curriculum issues; close contact with the Registrar's office about GSLIS curriculum and registration issues; and contact with students about their courses. For communications, I oversee the GSLIS Web site content and GSLIS print publications and work with other staff members on communications with alumni and the professional community. Daily tasks in this part of my job include working with the college's Web Office on how the site reflects the program while also fitting into the overall Web site architecture; serving as managing editor of our monthly newsletter—assigning stories, leading the team producing the newsletter, making final decisions on content, and doing outreach; overseeing GSLIS print publications—choosing, managing, and supervising the writers, designers, and photographers, managing the content, gaining approvals; and working closely with other college staff to produce our alumni publications.

Having a background in the field helps me produce better materials and understand how to present the program well. And I hope that what I bring to my job—including the memory of being a student in this very program—helps our students have a better experience. Organizational skills are obviously key; knowing the pedagogical underpinnings and where faculty are coming from when they discuss the curriculum is also an important part of my job. Before going to library school, I spent seven years planning conferences and events. The job I have now brings both those paths together.

Being in a library school makes it easy to keep up with professional publications, but I also listen to the students as they're always looking at things in a completely fresh way—it's inspiring! I love that I can have this wonderfully challenging and fulfilling job, but also have the flexibility I had hoped for. I like least that I never have a snappy enough comeback when people say, "But you're not a *real* librarian."

Jen Doyle is Director of Curriculum and Communications, Simmons College GSLIS, Boston.

Endnotes

1. Julie Jansen, *I Don't Know What I Want, But I Know It's Not This: A Step-by-Step Guide to Finding Gratifying Work,* New York: Penguin, 2003: 9.
2. Julie Harwell, "Training Resources Manager," in Priscilla K. Shontz and Richard A. Murray, eds., *A Day in the Life: Career Options in Library and Information Science,* Westport, CT: Libraries Unlimited, 2006: 309.

Chapter 3

Organizations Similar to Libraries

Your own career is an investment you make in yourself, one that—unless it is interrupted or derailed—will pay dividends throughout your life. Some benefits are financial, some are intellectual or creative, and others involve different kinds of personal growth.[1]

You can continue easing your way into alternatives by looking at careers with organizations that are in some way similar to libraries. Many types of institutions, organizations, and companies resemble libraries, devoted in their own way to education, preserving and disseminating information, books and reading, or other typical library-related activities. Library skills, background, and education transfer directly and obviously to these fields, allowing you easily to market yourself as a viable candidate and to find success without having to completely retool your skills. This sense of familiarity can be reassuring to those who love the library environment or mission and wish not to range too far from the field. When making a major life change, it can be reassuring to work from a solid foundation and keep some base of familiarity—in this case, the mission, job duties, or work environment.

As discussed in Chapter 1, identifying your current goals and the reasons you initially chose library work can help you identify alternative careers that match those goals and reasons. Think back to these when considering which related organizations might be a good fit. Think also about how similar organizations not mentioned here might match your own priorities and reasons for choosing libraries. The following sections are far from exhaustive, but simply suggest some possible directions for your search.

Bookstores

The core mission of libraries generally differs from that of for-profit institutions such as bookstores. However, librarians who enjoy working around books, matching the right book to the right reader, sharing their love of books and literature, championing the right to read, and planning author-related and other events can still find a fantastic fit in the bookstore setting. People often enter librarianship, at least in part, out of a love of the written word; you can continue to scratch that itch by working around books in a retail environment. Again, the rightness of this fit depends in part on your initial reasons for pursuing library work, as well as your personal preferences and priorities.

Opportunities for work in bookstores range from finding a job at a major national chain like Borders or Barnes & Noble (perhaps a temporary position while you continue to seek full-time library work) to lending your expertise to an independent bookstore to starting a rare books business over the Internet. Librarians' expertise with both books and people comes in handy in any of these contexts. Directly transferable skills and experience may include:

- Bibliographic knowledge built up over years of working in libraries

- Book and author promotion

- Children's programming skills, including conducting storytimes, booking performers, lining up character costumes, and arranging author visits

- Collection development experience, including knowledge of popular materials

- Commitment to intellectual freedom

- Creating displays

- Customer service skills, including the ability to deal with difficult people, get to the heart of what a customer is looking for, and serve each person equally

- Dealing with publishers and distributors

- Marketing

- Reader's advisory

- Reference interview experience

- Research skills

The ongoing consolidation of the bookstore business and the predominance of a few national chains, plus ever-increasing competition from Amazon.com and other online outlets, do make bookselling—especially independent bookselling—a less lucrative prospect than it once was. Be sure to get a realistic picture of the current market before making the jump. Idealizing the bookstore of 20 years ago is as unproductive as idealizing the library of the past.

Useful organizations, conferences, and resources for booksellers include:

- American Booksellers Association (ABA), www.ambook.org

- BookExpo America, www.bookexpoamerica.com

- BookSense.com, www.booksense.com

- *Publishers Weekly*, www.publishersweekly.com

- *Shelf Awareness*, www.shelf-awareness.com

While librarianship is a less-than-highly paid profession, the job of bookstore clerk has us beat hands down. In many cases, these types of positions pay barely more than minimum wage, and often the only opportunities available are part-time, with no benefits. You may, though, be able to parlay your library experience or degree into a supervisory or management position in a bookstore, which can offer more opportunity for advancement, more chances to use your library skills, more opportunity to learn the ins and outs of the business, and better benefits.

Again, be able to show how your skills, education, and background would transfer, and think about what you want out of this job. Are you just seeking a part-time job as a supplement to your library career? Do you want to learn the ropes so that you can later open your own store or move up into bookstore management? Are you looking for a job to tide you over while you continue to seek full-time employment in a library, or are you thinking of making a career out of this type of work? Your answers will determine both the type of work you will accept and your focus in your new career.

If you do wish to make a career out of working in a bookstore, you may wish someday to open or invest in your own. Owning a bookstore is a secret (or not so secret!) dream of many librarians, whether it's starting your own store or taking over an established business. If you do want to own a bookstore, start by getting a job in a bookstore—preferably an independent bookstore. This may be a part-time job in addition to your current library career (especially given the low pay inherent to the bookstore market) but the best way to learn the ins and outs of the business is through on-the-job training. Think of this as an old-fashioned apprenticeship. We truly learn by doing, and, just as in librarianship, the sheer love of books isn't enough to turn us into professionals.

If you plan to open a new bookstore, be prepared to do your market research to determine whether your target area can support a bookstore and what kind of competition you might face from existing establishments. Do you want to combine a bookstore with one or more other ventures, such as a coffee shop, perform-ance venue, bar, tea room, or Internet café? Might your store engage in related activities, such as publishing a local literary mag-azine or email newsletter, sponsoring poetry slams, or displaying and selling local art? Will you offer storytimes, book local perform-ers, host author visits, sponsor book groups? Will you specialize in a specific type of literature (children's, mysteries, graphic novels and manga)? Will you sell used books, new books, or both? What related merchandise might you stock?

Think about factors like location, what you might specialize in, and how you will market your venture to the local community. When opening a small, independent bookstore you will likely need to be a jack-of-all-trades, responsible for everything from creating the store's Web site to conducting storytime to doing the books to manning the cash register, but marketing will be the most impor-tant component. You can think outside the box here: One survey respondent who sells books at medieval and Renaissance festivals shares: "Most of the time, I am a bookseller. During the week I do all the things any bookseller does—order material, maintain inventory, look for new items to stock, bookkeeping, etc. On week-ends, I dress in a period scholar's costume (robe, biretta, hose), hawk my wares, and sell books, plus reproductions of period play-ing cards, maps, prints and the like."

If you are considering buying an existing bookstore, look at its sales patterns, its traditions, the relationships the store has devel-oped with its local community, and how you might continue and strengthen these ties. Independent bookstores obviously can't beat the chains on price, so your advantage lies in exceptional customer service, local connections, and the urge to share your passionate knowledge of books. In 2006 alone, 97 ABA member bookstores opened (news.bookweb.org/news/4955.html), belying the popular perception that independents are a dying breed.

Anyone interested in opening an independent bookstore should begin by visiting the ABA's "Opening a Bookstore" site (www.book web.org/education/opening). Read and ponder the information provided there, then request a kit on the subject. A couple of times a year, the ABA also offers five-day workshops titled "Prospective Booksellers School" (www.bookweb.org/education/opening/ prospective.html)—again, a fantastic way to get introduced to the ins and outs of the business. Other resources for prospective booksellers include the ABA Emerging Leaders Project (www.aba emergingleaders.org) and Paz & Associates—The Bookstore Training Group (www.pazbookbiz.com). See Chapters 4 and 5 for more on starting your own business.

Other options include specializing in rare books or first editions, but again, the Internet has brought tremendous change to the rare books business model, in many cases cutting out the middleman. Creating a viable business will require a great deal of time and effort on your part, as well as a great deal of knowledge about the value and condition of rare books. Also important are the relationships you build with other dealers and sellers. You might particularly seek a career in rare books if you have experience in materials preservation and conservation or some background and knowledge built up through related archival work.

Publishing

Many librarians make a successful leap to the publishing world, whether in a part-time, freelance, or full-time capacity. (Find more on the related options of freelance writing and book reviewing in Chapters 4 and 7.) You may be able to turn your library experience into work either with a library-related publisher or with a general or academic publisher; your knowledge of the book market and your professional experience are both assets here. If you currently work in an academic library, you might start by seeing if your institution has a university press. Go meet the people there; offer to volunteer your services.

Book publishers range from large to small, from megaconglomerates to independent presses, from regional publishers to academic presses, and from professional to trade publishers. Each has its own mission, its own priorities—and its own problems! And, each will offer a different working environment and focus. Jobs in publishing include marketing assistant, sales representative, acquisitions editor, copy editor, indexer, managing editor, rights and permissions manager, and more. Each position requires a different mix of talents, and a different type of personality.

If you are looking to work from home, consider becoming an acquisitions editor. A nice perk about that position, in particular, is that publishers often allow acquisitions editors to telecommute, preferring to attract the best candidates rather than just those in a particular geographical area. Electronic communication facilitates this option; editors can easily keep in contact with both their publisher and their authors via email, online chat, and phone. You may wish to start by exploring opportunities with library science-related publishers, especially if you have a background writing in the library field and contacts at professional publishing houses or magazines. If you think you might eventually want to pursue publishing as a career, you can also build up your resume by taking on volunteer or part-time opportunities, as an association journal editor, a referee for a peer-reviewed publication, or a newsletter editor. (These types of positions generally do not pay, except perhaps in the form of reimbursement for conference attendance, but they will help you develop as a professional, regardless of whether you eventually choose to leap into the publishing field.) Any publishing experience will be useful, both inside and outside the field. Think about taking a course or workshop; explore opportunities like the ALA WNBA Eastman Grant (www.ala.org/ala/ourassociation/publishing/alapubawrds/wnbaannheidbreder.htm), which provides up to $750 for a librarian to take a course or participate in an institute devoted to aspects of publishing as a profession.

You can also consider pursuing a career in magazine, journal, or newspaper publishing. Be aware, though, that many newspapers prefer applicants to have a degree in journalism, and that entry-level jobs, especially at smaller outlets, are notoriously low paying.

The job-hunting process in publishing relies especially heavily on networking, and your professional contacts will continue to prove invaluable in your new career. Your personal network provides you with go-to people for quotes, insights, and advice, as well as potential authors for your publication or your publishing house. Watch the library job boards, as well as relevant email lists, for announcements of jobs in library-related publishing. These often stress professional networks and library expertise over, in addition to, or in lieu of specific education or background in publishing. Representative ads from summer 2007 include language such as: "… candidate must have broad knowledge of libraries and librarianship and library and information science. A specialty in school and children's/YA librarianship is a possible plus. Experience in acquisitions or other aspects of publishing is greatly preferred but we will consider other candidates with strong professional knowledge and networking."

There is really no formal academic career plan for either book or periodical publishing. The field often draws from English or journalism majors, but publishers are used to incorporating people with different backgrounds and education. If you feel the need for further education, you can pursue a number of relevant masters, certificate, or continuing education programs (classes in copy editing, proofreading, etc.). Transferable skills, useful background experiences, and personal traits for work in publishing include:

- Ability to express oneself clearly, both in writing and in person

- Attention to detail

- Familiarity with the peer review process

- Imagination and ideas

- Knowledge of the library market, key conferences, and ways to reach librarians

- Knowledge of what people want to read

- Love of the written word

- Management skills

- Marketing experience

- Organizing/cataloging (layout/navigation, creating a catalog, organizing titles on a PC)

- Reference/research abilities

- Sales skills

- Subject specialty

- Technology skills

- Willingness to work more hours than a regular 9-to-5 job

- Your own experiences with the publishing industry as an author and or/purchaser

Again, you will need to adjust your attitude and your expectations to work in a for-profit (even if little profit!) environment. Be prepared to have projects you find personally fascinating rejected due to their lack of marketability.

Jobs in publishing include everything from editor to fact checker to literary agent to story analyst. Lori Cates Hand's Publishing Careers blog (publishingcareers.blogspot.com) often contains interviews with people working in various aspects of publishing as well as advice on breaking into the field. Additional resources for those seeking a career in publishing include:

- BookExpo America, www.bookexpoamerica.com

- mediabistro.com job listings, www.mediabistro.com/joblistings

- *Publishers Weekly*, www.publishersweekly.com

Pursuing Publishing

My whole life has led up to being a publisher. I was copy-editing chief for my college paper and editor-in-chief for its literary magazine; I have been a writer since age 6. My work with teens involved teaching them to write, including creating a teen art and literature magazine for my former library. Acquiring materials over 11 years of working in libraries also helped me understand the publishing industry, from the perspective of a buyer needing to catalog books so that people could find them. In the end, I think publishing chose me.

In addition to all the editor stuff (reviewing manuscripts, procuring illustrations, laying out books), I hire myself out to libraries and present writing workshops for teens. I design workshops around many different topics and tailor my services to each library's needs. This lets me help not just one group of teens at one library, but many teens at many libraries.

I see great opportunities for collaboration on teen advocacy. I still post on library discussion lists, socialize with former colleagues, have good relationships with librarians where I present workshops, and attend conferences. It's a lot harder now that I have to pay for myself, but I'm hoping to increase my professional involvement as the budget allows. I do miss the daily interaction with teens and reader's advisory—however, I don't miss the daily hour-long commute, having to answer to someone else, clearing new ideas through a committee, and having to convince coworkers that teens matter.

Being my own boss is great, but I most appreciate seeing people's faces light up when they realize that I can help them make their dreams come true—particularly when that's a teen face. There are so few adults who really seem to be in their corner that I feel kind of like their champion. I'm saying, "Hey! I believe in you! Let's show the world how creative you really are!" For now, what I like least is the money. I started this company with my husband on what could be called a shoestring budget—on a good day! We're in our first year (second fiscal year), and I think we might just barely make a profit this year. I hope this will eventually become a full-time job for both of us, but finances are currently very tight.

I would tell people not to go out on their own if they aren't good at being their own taskmaster, or if they aren't good with business forms and taxes. I am extremely fortunate to have a husband who took a lot of business classes; he has been a tremendous help in handling tax forms, permits, invoices, and record keeping. At the very least, be sure to read a few books on the subject so you know what forms to seek out and file. Marketing myself is also new territory. I'm on a steep learning curve about remaining involved in library discussions without sounding like a constant advertisement for the Grumpy Dragon.

Getting my MLS taught me how to approach work as a professional. Being a professional publisher requires that same mature approach if you want people to take you seriously. Graduate school also taught me a lot about how librarians talk to each other. If you're going to be successful selling

books to libraries, you have to know how to enter that communication loop and keep a good reputation for service.

*Spring Lea Ellorien Henry is Editor/General Partner, The
Grumpy Dragon (www.grumpydragon.com), Colorado
Springs, CO.*

Another possible career path for librarians moving into the publishing environment involves specializing in sales to libraries. Here,
your knowledge of the library market is essential, as are your connections to professional associations and other librarians. Think
about your own comfort level here—sales work with publishers
resembles work with other library vendors, discussed in Chapter 2.

Freelance Services to Publishers

Publishers, especially book publishers, tend to outsource a
number of functions to freelancers, including indexing, copy editing, abstracting, and fact-checking, all of which easily utilize the
organization and technical skills of librarians. Cynthia J. Coan,
self-employed indexer, Indexing By the Book, Tucson, AZ, explains:
"Creating an index to a large extent involves putting oneself in the
mind of the reader. One has to be able to anticipate in advance the
terms under which a reader is likely to look up topics of interest.
This is crucial not only in compiling terms but also in determining
appropriate cross-references, activities which I had to perform on
a regular basis when doing cataloging. As for coming to know
one's readers well enough to anticipate their information needs
and predict their search strategies, reference, with which as long-
time solo librarian I also gained considerable experience, is definitely good preparation." Enid L. Zafran, owner, Indexing Partners
LLC, Lewes, DE, similarly notes that "Knowing how people seek
information and use information is a great skill for an indexer to
have. Indexing is more than just picking out words and getting

them into order. It brings organization to information and sets it in a framework. You need to think about what types of issues the book is about or the way someone would use an index in an electronic environment differently from doing a word search."

Few publishing houses employ full-time indexers; choosing this as a primary or supplementary career generally requires a comfort with both a freelancing lifestyle and an uneven workload. Freelance indexers are project-dependent, so they can be overwhelmed some days and twiddling their thumbs on others. This also means that your income will be uneven, so you need to do some serious planning and saving to pursue the freelance route. Indexers need a high comfort level with managing deadlines, as well as setting and sticking to a reasonable fee schedule.

Vendors often also employ indexers and abstractors, which can be a more viable path toward full-time employment (as opposed to freelancing); see more on striking out on your own and balancing its challenges in Chapters 4 and 5.

Some indexers focus on a particular subject area, allowing them to market themselves as experts whose knowledge of the subject matter allows them to create more accurate indexes. If you currently serve as a liaison to a particular academic department, have a subject specialty at your institution, or have a degree in another field, you can turn your subject knowledge into an indexing specialty. Market yourself as an indexer of medical texts, legal volumes, or professional materials. Resources for indexers include the American Society of Indexers (ASI; www.asindexing.org) and the National Federation of Abstracting and Indexing Services (NFAIS; www.nfais.org).

If your library school failed to include coursework on indexing, think about taking a class or otherwise educating yourself before taking the plunge (ASI offers a class, as do some schools and other organizations). If you intend to specialize in a given subject area, you'll also need to familiarize yourself with its terminology.

Micro-organizing

I practiced law for six years and found it stressful and contentious. I looked into indexing a bit then, and remember thinking I couldn't afford the training. I then spent two years working in circulation (which was fun, but boring) before moving into a law librarian position—which I love.

Now I have two little boys, so I began thinking about work I could do from home. I looked into indexing again, hooked up with a practicing indexer who teaches, and got going. I currently spend 27 hours/week at my day job, and anywhere from 0 to 20 hours per week indexing. It has actually built up faster than expected, and I may need to cut down on it or quit the day job soon.

As a freelance indexer, I take on projects from publishers or book packagers. I read the book carefully and construct an index, primarily using the author's terminology but also other likely synonyms to provide multiple access points. The index should include all the main terminology, but also address the ideas and themes in a book. So you are indexing both words and concepts. Indexers organize information and help people find it. Librarianship is the macro level, and indexing the micro level.

I like that indexing is challenging. It requires more mental concentration than my day job. It makes good use of my type-A side, and I can take or refuse jobs according to my schedule. The pay is pretty good, because I'm actually pretty quick at it. What I like least is that sometimes the book schedules slip—they tell you that they will have a 500-page book to you on April 1, and it's due back on April 15. Then, you hear that they think it will actually show up April 8, which pushes everything back and possibly runs into other projects. It's also lonely work—you do it at home by yourself. That's one reason I haven't quit the day job!

My legal background comes in very handy; it's hard to index legal materials without being familiar with the language. I work in a law library and do some legal indexing, so I see how people use actual indexes and what blocks they run into, and try to address that in my work. The more you read and are educated, the easier it is to index, as you draw from everything you know. I had to learn all the basics of indexing, and then I had to learn to trust myself to just figure out what I didn't know—you learn the concepts, but applying them is a very grey area, in which the answer is very often "it depends." I have a hard time with that, and have to work on just making a decision and moving on.

Anyone interested in freelance indexing work should first get involved. Join a local indexer group if you have one, go to local or national meetings, and get to know people. You will learn more about indexing that way, you will have people you can ask questions of, and you will get referrals.

Maria Sosnowski is a Freelance Book Indexer, Portland, OR, and Law Librarian, Clark County Law Library, Vancouver, WA.

Cynthia J. Coan, who took a self-paced distance course before launching her indexing business, continues: "Never overlook the importance of formal training and/or coursework. It cannot only mean the difference between landing a job or not in one's newly chosen field, but is also the best way to ensure achieving quality performance in a new field."

Abstracting is another possible career path, and database vendors and publishers both hire abstractors. Writing an effective abstract requires the ability to distill complex material down to its essence, and again draws on your organizational, analytical, and communication skills. You can also put your attention to detail or your research skills to good use as a copy editor or a fact checker. Think about where your own strengths lie when looking at potential freelance work with publishers.

Education

While teaching in LIS programs (which was discussed in the Chapter 2) is one career option, an entire world of education-related employment options also awaits you. Think about teaching adult education classes at your local community college, or doing computer training at your local technology center. Make use of your background in bibliographic instruction, presenting, instructional design, or technology training. If you have specialized in a certain subject area or served as a liaison to an academic department, you can use this subject knowledge in your search for teaching opportunities. If you have a BA in a particular subject, a second masters, or a PhD in another discipline, combine this with your background in library work to market yourself as a skilled researcher and trained professional.

A background in youth services or school media librarianship might lead you to become an elementary, middle school, or high school teacher. Some areas in desperate need of teachers offer a fast-track education degree that you can earn on the job while using your relevant skills in the classroom, and some of your school media coursework may transfer toward the degree. Private schools that don't require state certification for teachers might also be very interested in your background in libraries, information literacy, and working with children. Again, libraries and schools have parallel missions, both seeking to educate and inform. Show how your library experience will allow you to work well with the school's librarians, and talk up how you will integrate the library's services into your coursework, help guide students to useful resources, and teach them to evaluate sources.

You can also parlay your skills in training and bibliographic instruction into becoming a corporate trainer or a developer of online courses and tutorials. Corporate training is similar to work as a trainer for a library vendor—only your target audience differs. You can develop online courses for librarians or for nonlibrarians, either marketing these yourself or hiring yourself out to a larger organization that provides these types of classes.

Related Institutions: Archives, Museums, and Historical Societies

Archives, museums, and historical societies directly resemble libraries in their focus on information, research, and preservation. They seek similar skills in their staff—and sometimes specifically seek degreed librarians. In most cases, a history or archival background will be useful here; if you have an undergraduate degree in a related field, this can also come in handy. You can also look for continuing education opportunities in archives, preservation, or related topics. An advanced certificate in a field like museum studies will be useful, as will certification by the Academy of Certified Archivists (www.certifiedarchivists.org/html/cert.html; note that this requires qualifying professional experience in addition to passing an exam). Alternatively, a commitment to the field demonstrated through relevant courses and workshops can help you make the jump.

Think about how your skills and background best transfer and what type of institution you are looking for. If you are looking into museum work, for instance, would you best fit into an art museum, a history museum, a science museum, or a natural history museum? If you are moving into archives, do you want to work at an educational institution, a business, a government archive, or a historical archive? Would you be best suited to working with digital media, manuscripts and letters, or photographs and film? Are you comfortable working on a short-term grant-funded project, or do you need more stability in your career?

If you are looking for work in an archive or a historical society, be sure to join your local historical society for networking and/or internship opportunities. Offer to volunteer at a local museum or historical society to gain some experience—most museums depend heavily on volunteers, and their volunteer coordinator will be happy to hear from you! Just as in libraries, work in these institutions comprises a number of specialties—museum work, for instance, includes everything from curation to collections, from administration to development, from archives to outreach. Each specialty requires a different set of skills. Also, look into additional national resources, including:

- American Association of Museums (AAM), www.aam-us.org/index.cfm
- Archives and Archivists (A&A) List from the Society of American Archivists, www.archivists.org/listservs/arch_listserv_terms.asp
- ARMA International, www.arma.org
- Aviso, Your Job Headquarters for Museum Careers, www.aam-us.org/aviso
- MUSEUM-L discussion list, home.ease.lsoft.com/scripts/wa.exe?A0=MUSEUM-L
- *The Official Museum Directory*, www.officialmuseumdir.com
- Society of American Archivists, www.archivists.org

In making the jump to this type of work, you will be competing with people who have specific backgrounds and education in museum studies, archaeology, history, or art history. Any experience or education in those areas will be useful, although ads often specify *either* a degree in the field *or* "related" education. One ad from summer 2007, for example, reads: "The successful candidate will have a Master's Degree in Museum Studies or a related field and 1–3 years experience in a museum environment. Experience working with and handling paper-based collections will be particularly beneficial." Another organization was looking for "a Web Archivist to assist in instituting a site-wide metadata scheme to facilitate access to electronic resources ... Academic library experience is a plus, but is not required."

Humanities backgrounds are fairly common among librarians, curators, and archivists, so also be sure to stress any special skills you bring to the table. These can range from fluency in multiple languages to digitization experience, depending on the position and the institution.

If you are leaving libraries to seek better pay, then museums, historical societies, and archives are probably not the place to look! All are notoriously low-paid, something you will encounter in many institutions similar to libraries. The job market is also tight in these fields, so if you are leaving librarianship due to a lack of jobs in your area, this may not be your next career of choice.

Some transferable skills and background for those moving into these sorts of related institutions include:

- Collection development
- Communication
- Conservation
- Preservation
- Research
- Technology

A Nice Synthesis

I came into the field with a master's in computer science. After high tech went south (at least in Boston), and there were lots of unemployed programmers, I noticed that the jobs I most wanted that related to digital projects often required an MLIS or being in library school. So, I went to library school.

Now, I work in public history in a publishing group in an historical society. I am working with two other people on a three-year grant-funded project to put the published volumes of the *Adams Papers* and the *Winthrop Papers* online. I work with less technical people to help with encoding, and I write the XSLT code that transforms the encoded text into the visible output.

I love everything about my career. I enjoy being in the history world, and am beginning a history PhD in the fall while I continue working on my project. I like working with TEI and with the XML and XSLT code. I love seeing the volumes come into existence online.

This is digital librarianship. Several of us who work in technical services at the Massachusetts Historical Society have an MLIS. We know how to work with collections, understand professional ethics, use our cataloging background to support good information architecture, and understand the key balance between access and preservation. Experience with rare books and archives is also very helpful in an historical society. Our management course has turned out to be helpful, something I wouldn't have expected. Collection development, cataloging, and other core courses make sense out of what we see every day in the world of publishing print-based and online materials. I need both my computer science training and experience and my MLIS to be successful; it's a nice synthesis.

I would never want to go back to high tech, even though my salary is two-thirds of what I made previously. I miss having more access to training and continuing education. Budgets for this are very tight in the nonprofit world, so I'm pursuing a PhD on my own at a nearby university to stay more current. I have support here for doing that, and a tuition waiver to fund it.

If you're interested in a similar career, find out about the institution and its mission, and talk with people who work there. I did an internship here, and it was the most valuable way I can think of to transition from library school to a satisfying job. Don't miss the chance to do an internship.

Our interns sometimes underestimate the technical proficiency needed for real-world online projects based on the exercises they do in classes. I wonder what messages library schools are giving about career expectations. People who want to work on digital projects need to take more challenging technical courses involving databases and be prepared to read a lot and practice on their own. There is a big gap between the people who come in with tech expertise, and those who got a little Web design, a little Access, some spreadsheets, and word processing as part of the MLIS. People should be able to cross-train for technology while in library school. I think this is very new territory for many of the existing faculty, which is why it's slow to be clarified.

Holly Hendricks is Technical Specialist, Massachusetts Historical Society, Boston.

Also useful is a familiarity with the general working environment and mentality of other organizations with philosophies and missions similar to those of libraries. Your library background helps you speak the same language and start off on the same page.

Nonprofits

Work with nonprofit organizations resembles library work in a number of aspects—and, again, generally in terms of low pay scales! In nonprofits as in libraries, a lack of sufficient funds to carry out targeted projects can be frustrating when trying to meet organizational goals or serve your community. Again, think about your own priorities and what you are looking for in your new career. If your reasons for moving on include low salaries and frustrations with constantly "doing more with less," nonprofits may not generally be the way to go, although this obviously differs depending on the organization and its success with grant writing, fundraising, and otherwise meeting its monetary goals. (Find more on work as a fundraiser or grant writer in Chapter 6, Information Work.)

These drawbacks aside, your work with libraries can be directly related to work with nonprofits. Transferable skills and background for the nonprofit environment include:

- Ability to stretch scarce resources
- Experience motivating others to work toward a common mission
- Experience with granting bodies
- Familiarity with government lingo
- Research skills

Your background in a specific area of librarianship can also prove useful: A health sciences librarian can transfer her skills to a public health-oriented nonprofit; a political science liaison to a public policy agency; an outreach librarian to a community outreach position; a reading specialist to a literacy organization; or a YA librarian to a youth organization.

Nonprofits can also resemble libraries in that you serve multiple constituencies with multiple agendas. Nonprofits have boards of directors, similar to those in most public libraries, and most must balance the interests of their community or constituency, major donors, board members, and other sometimes competing interests. Your experience in dealing with local politics and balancing various priorities will come in handy here, and nonprofit management resembles library management in many aspects.

Search for opportunities in nonprofit organizations at Idealist.org (www.idealist.org). If you wish to work in a nonprofit organization, a great way to begin is by volunteering your time, preferably at your targeted organization or in a related field, but any nonprofit volunteer experience should prove helpful and help give you a taste of what the work really entails.

Government

Librarians can move into relevant positions in every level and branch of government, and, in many cases, may find the working conditions and benefits remarkably similar to those in their former libraries. Here, your experience in one governmental organization directly transfers to work in another.

Researcher, analyst, records manager, and similar positions abound in U.S. government agencies, and your MLIS and/or library background can only be an asset here. (Find more on records management and other jobs working with data in Chapter 6.) Librarians outside the U.S. can find similar positions in their governments by using similar techniques and transferring the same skills, although the specific resources discussed here are largely U.S.-focused.

Search for U.S. federal government jobs at the official USAJOBS site (www.usajobs.gov). Relevant positions may or may not be listed under the term librarian, but often include terms like *analyst* or *specialist*. Consult the Federal Library and Information Center Human Resources Working Group publication "Looking for a Federal Information Job?" (www.loc.gov/flicc/wg/looking.pdf) for specific search strategies and tips. Language skills, a political science or history background, and a familiarity with other countries or cultures will also come in handy here.

You can also make the jump from library management to related careers in local government, such as municipal management. Moving into local government or into another city department will be easier if you have experience administering a local public library—especially the public library in the same jurisdiction. Administering any city department requires building partnerships with other administrators and local government officials, partnerships that you can carry over into a new role with the same municipality. Your experience directly translates, you already know the people and the politics involved, and you can continue your commitment to both public service and your local community. If you see this sort of move in your future, you may wish to pursue additional relevant education, such as a master's in public administration.

Other Related Organizations and Ideas

Research skills transfer to a number of other organizations, many of which may be delighted to snag a trained information professional. For instance, working in a library more than prepares you for work as a research assistant; however, you may face the curious mix of both being overqualified and dealing with a highly competitive environment (especially at prestigious universities).

Research assistants often engage in a mix of research and clerical work, so those pursuing this path can't regard this type of work as beneath them or as making insufficient use of their skills. You can also bring your research and analysis skills to organizations like think tanks, or provide research services to individuals. Doing research for individuals is similar to working as an information broker (see Chapter 5, Building a Business), but is generally done on a freelance basis. You can, for example, do research for writers of nonfiction or historical fiction, advertising your services or answering ads on craigslist (www.craigslist.org) or in magazines like *Writer's Digest*.

Another option is to utilize your research and detective skills by working as a professional genealogist. Especially if you work in a public library or specialized institution, you may already have direct experience assisting people with genealogical research. Even if you lack such experience, your research skills and respect for minutiae will come in handy. Resources include:

- Association of Professional Genealogists, www.apgen.org
- Board for Certification for Genealogists, www.bcg certification.org
- Genealogy Librarian News, genlibrarian.blogspot.com
- National Genealogical Society, www.ngsgenealogy.org

Any organization or area that requires research or works with information can benefit from the skills of a trained librarian. Your first job here becomes to sell your skills to your potential new employer.

Endnotes

1. Leslie Bennetts, *The Feminine Mistake: Are We Giving Up Too Much?* New York: Hyperion, 2007: 21.

Chapter 4

Striking Out on Your Own

Good intentions are important, but good action is better. So let's not talk so much about what we want to do, but instead start taking whatever steps we can right now to do what we most want to achieve.[1]

Librarians and info pros are often surprised to find they already possess a set of skills and knowledge that lends itself to self-employment; their marketable skills don't necessarily depend on a library infrastructure. While most librarians go into the field with the intention of working in libraries for the rest of their careers, the jump to working for yourself, especially if you stay connected to libraries somehow, can be less daring than it seems on the surface. Working for yourself also gives you the opportunity to stretch yourself professionally and to explore multiple fields—sometimes even simultaneously. As G. Kim Dority points out: "For independents, how many new and different ways are there to earn a living in an 'information-based' economy? The opportunities are essentially limitless, which is exhilarating on a good day—and often overwhelming on other days, especially for students!"[2]

The following sections outline some of the most common ways librarians begin to strike out on their own. You can, of course, use your unique mix of talents and skills to move in any direction you choose; don't be limited by what you read here, but simply use these ideas to consider possible directions. You will find advice and stories from others who have carved out their own path to self-employment, and you can also draw on some of the ideas in earlier chapters, such as indexing and abstracting, which are commonly done at home on a freelance basis.

Multiple Profit Centers

Librarianship has been described as the last refuge of the Renaissance person; your multiple interests lend themselves to moving in multiple directions. (In some cases, you can move in multiple directions at once!) These paths can be pursued independently, or woven together and combined with other activities to create what Barbara J. Winter calls *multiple profit centers (MPCs)*, or multiple streams of income that combine to create your new career. While pursuing several paths simultaneously makes it somewhat difficult to answer the cocktail party question "So, what do you do?", it also makes it easier to strike out on your own. You aren't reliant on a single income stream, and you can draw on multiple talents, strengths, and interests. As Winter explains:

> Rather than thinking in terms of having a single source of income (as we are trained to do when we see our income tied to a job), the savvy entrepreneur thinks about developing several income sources. With planning—and an openness to additional opportunities as they come along—you can create as many income streams as you desire. In time, you could be managing a great many enterprises, each earning a profit for you.[3]

Think in terms of both/and, rather than either/or. You can be a consultant *and* a writer; you can review books *and* travel around the country giving workshops to various groups; you can work in a library part-time *and* provide research services to fiction authors. Creating multiple profit centers doesn't equate to dabbling or failing to commit to any career path. Rather, it involves choosing more than one path on which to focus, with each path being a good match for your strengths and goals.

Your library background most likely prepared you to wear multiple hats, so carry this competency through to your new career path. Why place artificial limits on what you can do, on your job title, or on your career? Working for yourself generally requires that you rely less on job titles to define you, finding security in what you do, rather than what you are called. Multiple specialties can also make you more marketable. As Lori Erbs, Resource Consultant, Unlimited Resources, Acme, WA, says: "Especially in these days of budgetary cutbacks and radical global economic/social/political change, a person needs to wear a few different economic hats to survive. While librarianship has the tendency to breed specialization, it is critical for information professionals to learn auxiliary skills so as to diversify their employability."

Exploring multiple paths is also an option when a career- or self-assessment process shows you have strengths and interests in multiple fields. You can certainly pick just one or decide to explore these sequentially, but you can also choose to pursue more than one path at the same time.

Whether you identify one path or many, though, set some financial goals for your new business before striking out on your own. How much do you anticipate earning each month, after the first year of building up your business? Before taking the self-employment plunge, take the time to save up a nest egg to rely on while you establish your business, especially if you are your family's sole or main source of income. Ideally, bank six months to one year of living expenses if you intend to make the full-time leap. Take a realistic look at your expenses and finances; differentiate between necessities and luxuries, think about ways to conserve, and be prepared to accept a lower standard of living for some time. Striking out on your own will require a certain comfort level with the inevitable ups and downs and the irregular cash flow of self-employment, even after you are more established in your new career.

While it may be difficult to meet your financial goals through one type of work, you can ease the process by simultaneously meeting several smaller goals through these multiple streams of income. Let's say you live frugally or have a partner's income to draw on, and you want to earn $20,000 in your first year of self-employment. Rather than seeking to earn all $20,000 from one enterprise, you may find it less intimidating (and more realistic) to set a goal of $5,000 in consulting work, $5,000 in honoraria for speaking engagements, and $10,000 from part-time work at your current job. (Yes, your day job can also be a profit center!) Even if one path isn't as profitable as expected or builds less slowly than you'd hoped, you still have other areas to draw upon. It's often best to start your own business while still working a "day job," taking time to build both your reputation and your financial viability.

In this new career you are creating for yourself, then, you don't have to be limited to one type of work. If you initially chose librarianship because of an interest in finding out about multiple topics and taking on new challenges, you can use that same impulse to follow multiple paths. Carry your librarian-like curiosity with you as you strike out on your own; identify a variety of potential careers and interests to serve as your new profit centers. Your best mix of transferable skills and qualities here depends on your specific library background and on your intended self-employment path(s). These may include:

- Accurate record keeping
- Ability to deal with change
- Attention to detail
- Customer service experience
- Flexibility
- Managing budgets

- Managing people

- Marketing

- Multiple interests and varied knowledge

- Networking

- Organization

- Self-motivation

- Strategic thinking

- Technology skills

When deciding how and when to strike out independently, again, make an honest list of your own skills and attributes and think about how each transfers to your desired career(s). Be sure to go with your interests. If you are striking out on your own, you need to be both good at what you do and passionate about your career. Self-employment is not for the fainthearted.

If you do choose to pursue multiple paths, your answer to "What do you do?" depends on the context of the question. Since every encounter can be a marketing opportunity, you can choose to introduce yourself by listing one or more titles (author/consultant), or you can choose to present yourself wearing one particular hat. Target your bio and your introductions to the audience; if you're speaking to a group of librarians about a library-related issue, for example, your second career as a private investigator or life coach may be less relevant.

The following sections talk about some career paths that best lend themselves to freelance or blended work (although, with more time and effort, they can also each be built into full-time careers). Most of these you can jump into on a very small budget, working from a home office, so you won't need to invest heavily in startup costs. Working for oneself and from home can be a blessing in many ways for self-directed career changes. As Beth Gallaway, library trainer/consultant, Hampton, NH, explains: "My

Experimenting with Alternatives

I worked in a special library setting from 1993–1998, and, while I enjoyed the work, I had little patience for corporate politics or bureaucracy. I began to wonder if there was a way to still be involved in research and analysis, but independently. In 1999, I started my *first* alternative career as a freelance book indexer—primarily because I made some contacts in the industry and sort of fell into it. I left the corporate library environment and spent a year working as an indexer on a documentation project for Westinghouse while also growing my book indexing business. At Westinghouse I was one of a team of indexers evaluating and categorizing nuclear power plant documentation. Boring, but well paid.

In 2001, I took a part-time position as a hospital librarian, but at the same time was experimenting with other forms of independent alternatives. From 2003–2005, I wrote journal article abstracts for COR Health, a healthcare content producer. In 2005, I started teaching information literacy online for University of Maryland University College (UMUC). Late in 2005, one of the physicians at the hospital where I worked put me in touch with an attorney group doing medico-legal work, and I did a bit of freelance research and document delivery. In 2006, I started doing taxonomy and database management work for the Family Physicians Inquiries Network (FPIN) and in 2007 landed a course development contract for Drexel University. I still work for UMUC and FPIN, as well as consult one day per week for the hospital library.

Here is what a week might look like:

Monday: Download 50 clinical questions from FPIN database into my local database; index using MeSH (Medical Subject Headings). Email Drexel IT department about getting

Captivate installed on my home PC. Write activity for new course I'm developing for Drexel. Have lunch. Go back to FPIN database and do a "duplicate check" of about 20 of the 50 new questions to make sure they don't exist in database of 3,500+ existing questions.

Tuesday: Make final edits on first draft of chapter I'm writing for edited volume on health literacy. Continue doing duplicate checks of remaining new clinical questions. Have 30-minute conference call with FPIN staff about status of new questions. Put final touches on new course proposal that I'm submitting to ACRL.

Wednesday: Find out if assigned readings for weeks 1–3 of new course are available via Drexel electronic journals; if not, see if I have them in personal collection. Make decision regarding required textbook. Work on grading rubric for activity I created on Monday.

Thursday: Work at hospital library. Go to grocery store.

Friday: Figure out why so many old questions have not been moved through the question editing process in the FPIN database; run duplicate and status checks on oldest questions and move them along in the editorial management system so that unique questions can become available to potential authors. Knock off early to read new novel and drink red wine.

I love that I'm not doing the same activity or process every day. I get bored very easily (went to three undergraduate schools, and had three or four majors; my average time in a job is 3.5 years), so working for a variety of folks in multiple fields is just plain fun. What I dislike is the isolation I sometimes feel working at home, and the ups and downs of life as a contractor. I also rarely have time to play with new technology or work on cutting-edge projects, because when I have a lull I'm usually busy trying to find new or more work.

The biggest piece of information I can offer is to never be afraid to ask for work. I can't count the number of times over the last five or six years when I've read a news release or a blurb about a new project or product and thought to myself, "Boy, they could really use an (indexer, searcher, editor, whatever) on that project." I almost always drop the parties involved an email, letting them know of my interest. Nine times out of 10 absolutely nothing happens, but a few times I've received interested replies. Both my FPIN and Drexel jobs came about because I expressed interest at the right time.

Marcy Brown is Consultant, Envision Research, Delmont, PA.

previous job was 63 miles from home, and after two and a half years of the back and forth I couldn't take the commute anymore. I loved my telecommute days, finding I was very self-directed, and wished I could always work from home. When the speaking engagements began coming in, I dropped to 30 hours a week to travel and talk. It wasn't enough." Cynthia J. Coan, self-employed indexer, Indexing By the Book, Tucson, AZ, shares similar sentiments: "I like having lots of autonomy and the freedom to set my own hours. During busy times, life can admittedly get a bit hectic as I battle deadlines. On the other hand, working for myself means that during slow times I can meet a friend over a leisurely lunch or spend time at the community garden where my mother and I have plots, things one can't so easily do during a weekday if one has to conform to an employer's hours."

Chapter 5 expands further on the topic of self-employment, discussing entrepreneurship in general, ways to build your work into a full-time business, and the nitty-gritty details involved in self-employment. It also includes some options that lend themselves better to full-time businesses than to either work on the side or a blended career.

Freelance, Contract, and Consulting Services

The line between freelance, contract, and consulting work is very thin, and many people use the terms interchangeably. However, as a general rule, freelance work is usually very short-term and involves a defined project; contract work often involves a longer-term commitment and more complex activities; and consulting generally involves work at a more strategic level. In each case, you are providing outsourced services to libraries, but be aware of differing terminology and perceptions when choosing what to call yourself.

Those making the leap to nontraditional work often begin by offering freelance services to libraries and related institutions, which can include options such as storytelling or providing adult or children's programming. Similarly, you can offer contract services such as teaching a library's public computer classes or doing its Spanish-language cataloging. These types of activities can often be successfully pursued in addition to your existing full-time job.

You can also share your expertise by providing various types of consulting, both to libraries and to related organizations. Possible career paths for librarian consultants include: becoming a marketing consultant, consulting on building projects, doing strategic planning, specializing as a consultant for schools or school media centers, becoming a library system or state library consultant, consulting on referenda, creating a library's online content or tutorials, and becoming a technology consultant. (Find more on related fields like information brokering in Chapter 6, Information Work.) Many people combine these ideas, offering several types of consulting that best match their own background and expertise, or serving as a consultant to a group that wants to get an entire new library off the ground.

Consultants, freelancers, and contract workers work on a project basis, allowing them some control over their own workflow. This arrangement can allow you to match your work life to the goals you set in Chapter 1—with one caveat: If you say "no" too often, your clients may look elsewhere. If one of your goals, for instance, is to have summers off, or be able to take extended vacations with your family, you can purposely choose to avoid taking on large projects during certain times of the year. If you are targeting a certain income goal, you can play with your rates, accept more work, add additional lines of work, and/or work more hours.

This type of work can often be more productive, not to mention lucrative, in combination with other activities. Speaking and writing on related topics, for example, can help build your reputation as an expert and generate a network of contacts. Keeping your day job can offer you currency and credibility when working on consulting projects that resemble your on-the-job duties. Focus first on areas in which you have previously found success. If you are a former library director who has led one or more large and successful referenda or building projects, market yourself as a referendum or building consultant. If you are a systems librarian with experience setting up networks or designing Web sites, market yourself as a technology consultant.

Transferable skills and background for freelancers, consultants, and contract workers can include:

- Experience with large-scale projects (building projects, referenda, technology planning, etc.)
- Fluency in one or more foreign languages
- Programming experience
- Research
- Strategic planning
- Technology skills

Any area in which you have experience can be useful, just as it proved useful to your current or ex-institution. You also have the advantage of an outside perspective, allowing you a certain objectivity that those working in the environment may lack.

Some of the most common consulting practices include major projects on which libraries might not have in-house expertise, while common contracting practices include long-term provision of outsourced services such as programming or cataloging. Planning consultants help libraries create long-range, strategic, or technology plans. You can also help plan the design of a new library building or addition, or plan the best way to achieve a successful referendum. Libraries often hire consultants to help them through a building project because they lack the in-house expertise and/or the time to do it themselves. Those who have built up their own expertise by implementing a successful building project in their own institution will be most in demand; consultants in this field are most often former directors, project managers, or administrators who have personally been through the process. Be sure to peruse *Library Journal's Library By Design* supplement and annual architecture survey, and *American Libraries'* annual architectural and design issue for an idea of the range of opportunities in this area.

You have a number of options when striking out on your own. Contract programmers, for instance, plan, conduct, and/or oversee an entire season of library programming, while freelance program providers come in to personally conduct a one-time program. Many librarians have gained direct experience providing programming to either adults or children. Working as a contract or freelance programmer lets you market that experience, hiring yourself out to do similar programs, either to smaller libraries that lack in-house staff or expertise, or to larger libraries wanting to expand their options by hiring outside performers.

Consultant for Positive Change

I have always been interested in architecture and buildings, working for a number of years as a general laborer and later as a union carpenter. To this day, I work almost continuously on the restoration of my historic home, doing most of the non-electrical, non-plumbing work myself.

While I was Lehman Librarian at Columbia University in 1977, they developed plans to merge the Whitney M. Young, Jr. Memorial Library of Social Work into the Lehman Libraries space, which required significant interior renovation. I was the only person on the Columbia University Library faculty with experience in the building trades who could read blueprints and communicate with tradespeople and contractors; therefore, I was designated Project Manager. From there, I was recruited to Queens College to assume the position of Chief Librarian, where a significant part of my responsibilities involved the planning and design of the Benjamin S. Rosenthal Library and the Music Library. I then moved to the University of Nevada, Las Vegas, where I served as Dean of University Libraries and was active in the design of the Lied Library and the Architecture School Library.

I have always been very entrepreneurial and intrapreneurial, setting up a number of revenue generating programs in the libraries I served. In the late 1980s, I became actively involved as a library facilities planning and design consultant, making the transition to doing it full time pretty seamless—if not exactly painless. I take enormous satisfaction in the fact that buildings that I planned and helped design more than 20 years ago are still referred to as "the new library on campus." I watch them evolve as needs and technology change, and I enjoy delivering a product resulting in a tangible object that can continue to exist, serve, and satisfy for more than 100 years.

Library buildings are our silent partners in delivering library services. Most library design is inadequate because we, as a profession, are too often content to replicate the successful forms of other organizations rather than thinking about what our constituents really *need*. We tend to hold on to forms and structures long after they have slipped into obsolescence or worthlessness because we are too afraid of making a mistake. So, as a planner, designer, seminar leader, writer, and facilitator, I believe that I perform a vital function that few others in the profession are doing. I view myself, in the words of former colleague Rebecca Riley, as a "catalyst for *positive* change." A surprising number of architects have little understanding of what libraries actually do and almost no awareness of what they can accomplish. So, my understanding of library operations, the research process, scholarly communication, library technology, instruction, and how people use and experience their buildings enables my work.

I most appreciate that my projects have a beginning, a middle, and an end, as opposed to academic administration where things are often started but never really finished. I like making decisions rather than talking about making decisions. I like that I answer directly to people who are empowered to act, such as college and university presidents, vice presidents, and academic officers. I do not especially like the endless travel, nights in hotels in different cities away from my wife, or eating by myself while on the road. I am terrified of getting sick while I am out of town, so have become something of a germaphobe, routinely wiping down all of the touchable surfaces in my room with antiseptic wipes.

As a small business owner, I am also responsible for all of the operations of my business. I spend significant effort marketing my services, which I do through direct referrals by satisfied clients, being hired repeatedly by architectural firms, writing articles, giving speeches and presentations, and sometimes pleading piteously for work. As a consultant, I work closely with librarians and with architects and engineers who look to me to guide the planning process and serve as a communications facilitator between different client/providers who may not fully understand one another's jargon and work. That is the glamorous part. Then, add in the need to maintain accurate files, do the correspondence, pay the bills, recruit and oversee staff, update and expand marketing materials, fix the machinery, and clean the office and empty the trash, and I end up with about a 90-hour work week, 51 weeks or more a year.

Small business ownership is not for the faint-hearted; it is rife with uncertainties and risk. I must constantly be aware of "opportunity costs," which are defined as the "cost in forgone alternatives." Given the choice between making a $2,000 down payment on a car or traveling to make a presentation before a prospective client, my car's appearance becomes secondary. So, planning, analyzing, and deciding are a major part of my work—a bad decision can put me out of business just as effectively as doing a bad job for my clients.

If contemplating this path, do as much reading in architecture, architectural practice, and construction management as you can. Work in a leadership capacity on several building projects before trying to market yourself as a library facilities consultant. Save your money. You will probably go through all of your savings, cash in your 401Ks, max out your credit cards, and borrow from Mommy and Daddy before starting to actually earn a decent living. All of the things you consider "essential" now, such as cell phones, a nice newish car, regular vacations, meals in nice restaurants, book club memberships, pleasure travel, superfluous professional memberships, and ALA conference participation, are actually non-essentials.

Matthew J. Simon, MLS, Associate AIA, is Dean of University Libraries, Delaware State University, and President, pre-DESIGN Planning Associates, Inc.

Contract catalogers provide outsourced cataloging for libraries. Work as a contract cataloger is most viable if you have a marketable skill such as fluency in one or more foreign languages that the libraries you target may lack in-house.

As a marketing consultant, your library background lets you understand libraries' unique needs and audience. You can apply your previous experience in running a summer reading program, going for a successful referendum, planning and advertising programs, or increasing attendance at your library toward helping other libraries develop viable marketing plans. Resources for library marketing consultants include the *Marketing Library Services* newsletter (www.infotoday.com/mls) and the American Marketing Association (www.marketingpower.com).

Automation consultants use their experience and technical skills to help libraries through the process of implementing or migrating to a new automation system. Libraries generally post an RFP (request for proposal) when engaging in this sort of large-scale project; watch for these on relevant email discussion lists such as PUBLIB (lists.webjunction.org/publib) and SYSLIB-L (listserv.buffalo.edu/archives/syslib-l.html). Create a Web site that outlines your expertise with particular systems; see if your state library or association maintains a list of automation consultants and find out how you can be included. Automation consulting will be an especially good path if you have previously managed a system migration. Some libraries also outsource other technology-related activities, most often Web design or IT troubleshooting and maintenance, while other organizations outsource the creation of some or all of their Web content—a job that relies less on technical skills than on skills in research and writing. Alternatively, you can serve as a digitization consultant or other technology-related consultant; see where your own skills match apparent demand.

Writing

While few info pros make a full-time living from writing for publication, many do combine writing with either traditional or alternative careers (often including speaking, discussed later in this chapter, which tends to grows naturally out of publishing activities). Some have made the leap to other types of publishing, such as writing children's books, young adult novels, or mysteries (more in Chapter 7, Working in Very Different Roles), but most continue to "write what they know," publishing in the library literature on topics of interest to librarians. If you seek to include writing as one of your multiple profit centers, you'll want to focus on the non-peer reviewed, general library literature, which is more likely to offer monetary compensation for your work. Realize going in that the library market is not particularly lucrative. If you write books for librarians, you face an inherently limited audience, where sales of more than 1,000 copies are considered decent (you do the math!). If you write articles for librarians, you're limited to the few outlets that pay—and would have to do an awful lot of writing to make this into a full-time career. Those interested in this path will almost certainly need to think about ways to combine their writing with other activities.

Writing for publication offers another refuge for the Renaissance person, who can find joy in researching and writing material on multiple topics. It's also a great outlet for the type of person Barbara Sher terms a "scanner," or someone "genetically wired to be interested in many things."[4] An author gets to use her work to explore a variety of subjects, thus avoiding both burnout and boredom.

It Worked Out

I fell into speaking engagements by virtue of being one of the first librarians to construct an index to the good stuff on the Web ("Best Information on the Net," originally known as "Where the Wild Things Are"). This gave me a reputation as an Internet guru, particularly one feature on the site (which I took with me when I left my job), "Neat New Stuff I Found This Week on the Web." I did a lot of training for local librarians and then branched out to state library associations, Internet Librarian, etc. The writing also came about accidentally. In 1996 I started writing a weekly column for a British online magazine; it was seen by an editor at Fox News Online, who offered me a weekly column—my first paid writing.

I realized then that: a) I was getting stale at my job; b) with my son making his own way in the world, I had nobody to support but myself; c) with a dirt cheap mortgage and no extravagant tastes, I was making enough with my writing and speaking to meet my basic expenses while I tried to make it as a writer; and d) if it didn't work out, I knew I could get another job.

It did work out.

Now, on Wednesdays, when there are no conflicting obligations, I construct *Neat New Stuff* and *ExLibris*, which I post on Thursdays. I spend November through January working on the "Movers and Shakers" issue of *Library Journal*. I do speaking engagements as they come along, and other writing as projects that interest me come along. What I like best is the freedom to select my assignments and do what I want to do when I want to do it. I promised myself that when I quit my job I would never again read a book out of duty, and I've been able to stick by that. I also like the fact that, not being tied to a job, I can follow the issues and challenges of the profession far more broadly than someone who has to squeeze their reading into the few minutes available during the workday, and thereby must focus on issues related to their current job. What I like least is that when you work alone, and have nobody living with you, you have to go out of your way to incorporate conversation into your life—and conversations by email, however enjoyable, are not sufficient.

My ability as a researcher is called on continually in my writing, as are my Internet skills. Every year, as I do "Movers and Shakers," I learn more useful tricks at file management— metatagging, loosely speaking. I did have to learn how to be an effective interviewer, and how to write for publication for both librarians and for ordinary readers. Basically everything I ever learned in my way-too-many years in college also turned out to be useful, along with my extraordinarily sticky memory. My MA in American civilization taught me how to stand outside my own culture to analyze it, which was help-ful when I wrote a column explaining the oddities of American life and culture. But it also allows me to look objec-tively at the profession I love and examine how (and whether) it's adapting to a rapidly changing electronic and demo-graphic environment.

If you're interested in doing something similar, build a base before you try to start. What I did worked because I was already known within the profession; I then expanded my reputation and usefulness to the profession by offering two ezines and other online services for free. The one thing I might have done differently, in hindsight, is wait one more year to quit my job to build my savings even further.

Marylaine Block, author of The Thriving Library: Successful Strategies for Challenging Times *(ITI, 2007), is a self-employed writer and speaker, Greensboro, NC.*

Writing for the library field allows you to draw on your professional background and contacts, and also allows you to keep up with professional issues and keep tabs on what's "hot." The process of writing for library publication in itself draws on many librarian-like skills and qualities, including:

- Analysis

- Communication

- Knowledge of the library market

- Love of the written word

- Personal experience with the issues

- Research

You can consider occasional unpaid writing to support your other activities—a professional blog, for example, can help focus your thoughts and organize your ideas, even though it pays in nothing but name recognition.

Book Reviewing

Book reviewing in the library field generally pays nothing. Pay for reviewing for popular magazines or newspapers ranges from nothing (except, sometimes, a copy of the book) to around $500—should you be lucky enough to become a book critic for a large urban newspaper such as the *New York Times*. Much has been written about the decline of book reviewing; realize that the future of reviews in national newspapers is less than assured—reviews tend to be a loss in terms of advertising revenue, and have less prominence in many places than they once enjoyed. However, online venues and databases are enjoying new prominence; reviewers and article writers for sites like NoveList do get paid, although not enough to cobble together an entire career out of reviewing.

You can, again, look at writing book reviews as a way to keep your hand in, if not as a money maker itself. If you work in a nontraditional field, think about volunteering to review titles in that field for a library-related journal; if you remain connected to librarianship, offer to review professional resources. Resources for reviewers include National Book Critics Circle (www.bookcritics.org) and GraceAnne Andreassi DeCandido's "How to Write a Decent Book Review" (www.well.com/user/ladyhawk/bookrevs.html).

Speaking

Skills in bibliographic or technology instruction transfer well to planning workshops and presentations for other librarians, and public speaking is another great choice for librarian types with multiple interests. While you repeatedly engage in the same activity, speaking or giving workshops, you can build expertise in multiple areas so as to offer presentations and instruction on a variety of topics. This keeps your research skills fresh and helps ensure you remain engaged and interested in your new career.

Your success as a speaker or trainer depends primarily on your name recognition and marketability. Get involved in association work, write for publication, and otherwise get your name out in front of others before making the plunge. Your network and reputation bring you the best opportunities. Beth Gallaway notes: "I have always wanted to work for myself. I was committed to giving back and sharing what I learned through my career, and that attitude led to invitations to write and speak—first locally in my consortium, then at a state library conference, then at ALA, and now for other state regional systems and libraries. Getting involved in ALA was key for me: I joined as a student, and Joel Shoemaker gave me my first appointment on the Organization and Bylaws committee. Being in YALSA gave me tons of opportunities to get my name out as a presenter and writer. I got my contact for the book I'm working on through someone I met at a Serving the Underserved training [session]."

As with most freelance work, your first speaking contracts and invitations will likely come from people in your network, who can also recommend you to others in their own networks. To gain confidence and experience, volunteer to present or serve on a panel at your local association meeting or offer to give a workshop for colleagues. The more often you present, the more confident and able you will become. Once you have given a couple of workshops and presentations, be sure to set up an online portfolio that highlights these; post some PowerPoint slides, audio, video, handouts, and/or links to workshop descriptions.

Resources for librarian speakers include the Liminal Librarian 2006 Speaking Survey results (www.lisjobs.com/blog/?p=68) and comments (www.lisjobs.com/blog/?p=69). You can also think about joining Toastmasters International (www.toastmasters.org) to gain public speaking experience and to get some valuable feedback. When you make part of your living from presenting or giving workshops, you need to begin treating this work like a business. Get all contracts in writing, laying out each party's responsibilities and your agreed-upon honorarium. Give some thought to pricing your services as a speaker, technology trainer, or workshop leader, which requires some forethought and willingness to ask for payment. We get so used to volunteering our expertise for library groups, and being sympathetic to the financial difficulties of our organizations, that it can be hard to

On the Loose!

Before striking out on my own, I was an academic librarian at Rensselaer Polytechnic Institute (RPI) in Troy, New York, for 17 years. I didn't choose my alternative career; it chose me! RPI offered "voluntary separation" packages to all employees. Since I was looking for a change, I decided to take the plunge—and the package. This was the kick in the pants I needed to get me moving. Though I had several job offers before I left, I opted to take a sabbatical and postpone my job search.

During my last two years at RPI, I taught a number of Internet- and technology-related courses for one of our regional library networks, and discovered that I really enjoyed teaching. When that library system found I was "on the loose," they asked me to teach more classes and administer their training grant. Through these classes I met librarians/administrators from many different library systems in the region. This led to more grants and teaching, and suddenly it seemed I had a business.

I hadn't planned for that! I was still watching the job ads, figuring I'd go back to a "real job" someday. But I was having a great time, meeting new people, learning more about the different facets of our profession, and being challenged to learn more about technologies and how they can be used in libraries. Besides, I still had some money in the bank from the separation package. That was such an important piece; it gave me the cushion I needed to take the risk of working for myself.

The most practical advice anyone ever gave me was to not underprice my time. You'll probably only be able to bill for 15–20 hours a week. The rest of your time will be spent developing new job prospects, networking, and doing administrative work and such. Bill accordingly—you need to make a living! Make sure you have money in the bank to tide you over when work slows down or your invoices get stuck in administrative backlogs. Find something you love doing and try it out while you still have a day job. Make connections with lots of people, you never know what might lead to an interesting new project. Don't take on something you know you can't deliver, but do take some risks. Even if you're not totally comfortable with a project, remember, as a librarian you know how to find out what you need to know and you know how to teach yourself new skills. You can do it!

Almost all of my work is grant funded. In some cases, I'm involved in writing the grants. In others, I'm hired to provide a specific service for an already funded grant. I develop and deliver technology-related training sessions to library staff throughout the Northeast. I've also developed Web sites for library systems and a number of special statewide resource sites for New York state libraries.

I love having the chance to work with so many interesting people, many of whom are now good friends. I also love having the freedom to pick projects that are interesting and challenging. Making my own schedule has had some nice personal benefits as well; I'm able to travel more than I would otherwise—and, when all the latest tech stuff turns my brain to mush, I can escape to the garden and pull weeds!

I least like dealing with the paperwork: invoices, billing, taxes, insurance, benefits, all the business-y side of things. And, to tell the truth, some days are lonely. If I don't have classes or meetings scheduled, I get a bit tired of sitting alone in my office. I often decamp to a bookstore, coffee shop, or library to use the wireless access, have a cup of coffee, and browse the new books.

I do miss daily contact with patrons and colleagues, including the close collaboration we had with the campus computer center staff at the college where I worked. There are times that I run into a tech problem or can't think of a way to accomplish something, and I wish I could call them up for some help. What don't I miss? Long staff meetings!

Polly-Alida Farrington is Consultant, PA Farrington Associates, Albany, NY.

ask for what we're worth. This can be an issue in any outsourced work for libraries or library-related organizations; you will need to overcome your natural sympathy and realize your own worth.

Again, speaking and providing professional workshops easily combines with other activities to create a patchwork career. Presenting combines especially well with writing. Speaking, writing, and freelancing or consulting blend easily in any combination, to create a new career or as add-ons to another career. Pursuing multiple related paths creates a natural synergy, each activity drawing on the others. Writing for publication makes you a better speaker; consulting work gives you plenty to write about. When creating your own path, think about ways to incorporate both/and, taking a librarian's curiosity and love of learning and letting it run free.

Endnotes

1. Paul and Sarah Edwards, *The Practical Dreamer's Handbook: Finding the Time, Money, and Energy to Live the Life You Want to Live,* New York: Penguin, 2000: 207.

2. G. Kim Dority, *Rethinking Information Work: A Career Guide for Librarians and Other Information Professionals,* Westport, CT: Libraries Unlimited, 2006: x.
3. Barbara J. Winter, *Making a Living Without a Job: Winning Ways for Creating Work That You Love,* New York: Bantam, 1993: 102.
4. Barbara Sher, *Refuse to Choose! A Revolutionary Program for Doing Everything That You Love,* New York: Rodale, 2006: vii.

Chapter 5

Building a Business

*What sort of a hazy designation is "information,"
anyway? Is it accurate to say that we simply "work
with" it? Wouldn't it be more on the mark to say
that we swim in it, we inhale it, we dream of it at
night?*[1]

Librarians often launch their independent career as a side gig, continuing to work their day jobs while also pursuing freelance, contract, or consulting opportunities. As time goes on, though, outside opportunities may tend to take over, leaving less time or focus to devote to that day job. As your second career grows—or if you wish to start out by taking that leap of faith—you can think about building your business into a full-time occupation, leaving your library job behind. If you have always dreamed of working for yourself, why not take that plunge? All of the skills and experiences you have built up, both in school and on the job, will be assets in your new career.

Advantages to self-employment include flexibility, the ability to be your own boss, lack of bureaucracy, and the fact that all of your hard work is for yourself. But you still have to love what you do! You need to have a real desire to work for yourself, not just the wish to escape a particular bad work situation. It will be hard; you'll need to deal with the inevitable ups, downs, and vicissitudes of self-employment, which will replace your existing workplace frustrations with a whole new set of issues.

For non-MLS info pros, self-employment also offers the opportunity to expand their careers without the roadblock of the degree hovering over them; build your business relationships outside of libraries, and you'll find nonlibrarians to be generally less than concerned about your degree status.

Needed and Wanted

I worked in libraries from 1971 to 1988, and then from 1995 to 1997. Now, I work on contract for government agencies with the main function of providing information to citizens and businesses. So, for example, I have researched the siting of small business/entrepreneurship centers in Ontario; I have provided content for a national Web site on exporting; I develop and give seminars on the export programs available in the province; I have taught the international trade research course for a national training organization; I developed and maintain a guide to online export sources for a provincial economic development agency; and I teach secondary market research at the local Entrepreneurship Centre.

I get business information to SMEs (small and medium enterprises) who usually don't go to the library. They don't go because the public librarians don't understand them and don't help them. Basically, I brief the entrepreneur on what to look for, what to ask for, and how to use the info when they find it. It's like special librarianship, but done in a public library context.

My work is an extension of librarianship—I bill myself as a "business information professional." I don't have an MLS (I have a post-graduate diploma in information science), and, though this was not a problem in the special library world, I had lots of comments from "real" librarians about my lack of traditional qualifications. Although I don't act as a librarian for these agencies, they recognize the library skill set and always introduce me as a librarian. They need and want me; the traditional library world doesn't.

I'd suggest anyone making a similar transition learn and practice all the soft skills, like presentation, budgeting, and marketing. I wish I'd made the leap much sooner, actually, and not suffered so long as a misfit in the traditional library world. My biggest transferable skill is marketing—I was a librarian in a major chemical company at a time of major downsizing and had to promote myself to stay employed. I still have to promote myself to stay employed, but now it's instinctive!

I'm very active in several library associations, as well as in my new market research field. I make a point of bringing back my nontraditional skills and passing them on to librarians who may use them. My latest effort is a session called "Making the Business Case." I miss the clients most—I just loved having weird engineering, chemical, patent, or management questions to research. I don't miss the hierarchy of traditional libraries, and the credentialism.

Maggie Weaver is Principal, Shaftesbury Associates, Ontario, Canada.

The following sections discuss the details of self-employment, developing that entrepreneurial mindset, expanding a freelance career into a full-time business, starting your own business as an independent information broker, and becoming a library vendor.

The Nitty-Gritty Details

When you work for yourself, you'll find you need to deal with a plethora of annoying details that your employer previously took care of, from taxes to accounting to marketing. Transferable skills to any form of self-employment must include organization, budgeting, and attention to detail.

First, you'll need to determine your form of business. The following very brief discussion (which just scratches the surface of this decision) applies to U.S. businesses, but your options are similar in most other places:

- If you stay small, want to keep things simple, and intend to keep working solo, you can operate as a *sole proprietorship*, doing business under your own name or a DBA ("doing business as"). This is the simplest form of business, but leaves you personally liable for any business debts and obligations.

- If you are going into business with someone else, you can consider formalizing a *partnership* agreement. Here, you will want to plan for multiple contingencies and spell out the terms of each partner's role: Will you be equal partners in terms of decision making and profit sharing? What will you call your business? What happens when one of you wishes to leave the partnership? Be sure to consult a lawyer, or at least a guide to creating these sorts of agreements, before proceeding.

- If you want to formalize things further, you can consider creating a *corporation* (in the case of small business, usually a *subchapter S* or *S-corp*), which has the main advantage of protecting your assets and reducing your personal liability. Business taxes for the S-corp are reported on your personal tax return.

- Your other option is an *LLC* (limited liability company), which provides some of the benefits of incorporation but keeps some of the flexibility of sole proprietorships or partnerships. LLCs are somewhat easier to set up than are corporations.

Use your research skills or talk to a lawyer to determine the right form of business for you. There are a number of useful titles from NOLO and other publishers that will walk you through the steps of choosing and setting up a business structure. Realize that as your needs change and your business grows over the years, you might wish to revisit this decision.

From the outset you'll need to keep accurate accounting records, which only get more complex as your business grows. You'll need to worry about taxes: In the U.S., self-employed people generally have to pay estimated income tax quarterly or face penalties at the end of the year, and you will be responsible for both your and your "employer's" share of payroll taxes, amounting to 15 percent of your earned income. Keeping accurate records is also important in determining what expenses are deductible. If you are working from home, make a special effort to keep your business expenses separate from personal expenses. Think about setting up a bank account and credit card that you use only for business purposes, or at least about entering your business-related expense receipts into a spreadsheet or accounting software like QuickBooks as soon as you make each purchase. Also think about whether you can work out of your home or whether you will need to rent office space. If working out of your home, look into the home office tax deduction. Find an accountant you can trust who will do both your personal and your business taxes.

Realize that as a self-employed person—whether you call yourself a contractor, a freelancer, or a business owner—you will lack most of the benefits that full-time workers in traditional organizations take for granted. These range from vacation time to health insurance to retirement accounts to pension plans. Such benefits generally account for an additional 30 percent over a full-time salary. Also keep in mind that your net pay when self-employed, after taxes and expenses, will be just about 50 percent of what you bill. In the U.S., health insurance is the elephant in the room, one big reason why more of us fail to take the leap into self-employment. Think about your options here, which include:

- Getting onto a spouse or partner's insurance plan.

- Investigating plans with a high co-pay and large deductible for use in emergencies.

- Looking at plans offered through (or mandated by) your state for low- and/or middle-income families. Illinois, for example, offers an All Kids plan for parents who don't have coverage for their children.

- Looking at plans specifically designed for small businesses. Some states mandate that private insurance companies provide affordable plans for small companies. Join your local chamber of commerce and talk to other small business owners to see what programs they are aware of.

- Maintaining temporary coverage through COBRA while you look for other options.

- Purchasing health insurance negotiated by a professional association, such as ALA (MARSH Affinity Group— Insurance for ALA members, (www.ala.org/ala/our association/membership/marshaffinitygroupinsurance information/marshgroupinsurance.htm) or the National Writer's Union (www.nwu.org/nwu/?cmd=showPage& page_id=1.3.18).

Your choices will depend on the options available in your state, whether you have children, and your current state of health.

Beyond health coverage, also plan for your own future and retirement, even if this seems quite far away at the moment. Self-employed individuals not only lack access to employer- or government-sponsored pension and retirement plans, but also to tax-deferred and employer-matching options like a 401k or 403b. A number of guides suggest ways to plan for retirement; basic planning for the self-employed includes strategies like maxing out your IRA contributions each year.

Your next big task will be to set your fees, or to determine a minimum hourly rate for which you are willing to work. Consider all the factors that go into running your own business—realize that you're personally paying for everything from office space (even if in your home) to benefits to supplies. Banish any lingering librarian squeamishness about the idea of making a profit or charging for your work—or for information! As Sarah and Paul Edwards explain: "We need to think of [profit] as our reward for making some valued contribution to the lives of those we serve. ... So, you must proudly charge what you know you're worth and make sure what you provide is well worth the price."[2]

Don't be afraid to ask for money, and don't undervalue yourself. You spent years acquiring the valuable skills you are now marketing to others, and when you accept less than you are worth you both undermine your own credibility and depress the market for others doing similar work. Guides to self-employment sometimes suggest beginning by charging double your last hourly rate in your previous position, which the market may or may not bear. While you can increase fees as you go along and build your business and your reputation, don't start so low that you undervalue your abilities and can't cover your costs. To get an idea of reasonable rates, use your network of contacts to see what others doing the same sort of work charge. See if anyone in your network, or anyone in their network, does similar work. Ask around and see if your potential competitors have posted price ranges online; investigate resources like the Editorial Freelancers Association (www.the-efa. org/res/rates.html), which compiles common rates as reported by members.

When working for yourself, as Ruth I. Gordon notes: "Remember that every minute you waste is your minute, not an institution's."[3] By the same token, every minute you're *productive* is your minute, not an institution's; everything you do is for yourself and your future. This can be both scary and exhilarating—think about where your own balance lies. As Mary Ellen Bates, owner, Bates Information Services, Inc., Longmont, CO, explains: "I really appreciate being able to try new things, set my own hours, and succeed or fail based on my own skills and efforts." Enid L. Zafran, owner, Indexing Partners LLC, Lewes, DE, concurs: "I enjoy the lifestyle that indexing and self-employment give me. I set my own schedule, I have no dress code, and I choose my own projects. I have no employees so I don't have the hassle that goes with employee supervision. When I work extra hard, the direct benefit goes to me, not some corporation. I am not bogged down with bureaucracy and playing corporate politics. When I want to travel, I can—I never have to ask for days off. And my work is very portable—I have worked in Europe, at a swimming pool, on planes and trains, etc., so I can go where I want, when I want, and still keep up with making a living."

Depending on the type and scope of your business, you will probably wish to create either a formal or informal business plan. This can help you see how viable your business actually is, and forces you to pay attention to all the little details you might otherwise miss in the excitement of your launch, including who your potential clients will be, how you will attract them, how you will price your services, your expected revenue for the next few years, and so on. The Small Business Administration (SBA; www.sba.gov) provides a useful small business planner Web site with sample business plans and step-by-step instructions (www.sba.gov/small businessplanner/plan/index.html) or you can look at any of the many step-by-step books on the subject.

Besides SBA, a good resource to help you make the self-employment plunge is the Service Council of Retired Executives (SCORE; www.score.org). Also check with your local community college or other educational institutions to see if they offer continuing education courses on the various aspects of running a small business, and check online for coursework on specialized enterprises such as research businesses.

Marketing Your Business

Effective marketing can be hard to wrap our heads around—it's hard enough to market our libraries, let alone ourselves! Yet, when you're self-employed, 50 percent or more of your efforts may be directed toward marketing, especially initially. Your success depends on your ability to get past your natural reluctance to talk up yourself and your services. Remember, you are striking out on your own because you believe in yourself and what you have to offer. Develop the confidence to convey that belief to others, which is another reason to build your career around your own passions and strengths.

Working for yourself is all about dealing with people, marketing being just one small part of this. If you went into librarianship with the idea of settling into a quiet, solitary career, going out on your own may be a bad choice. Get your "elevator speech" down pat, because anyone you talk to, especially at a conference or industry event, is a potential client. Be able to sum up your business and its advantages in less than 30 seconds.

Do your market research before you even start. Are others in your area offering similar services? What kind of a demand do you see? Do you have potential clients lined up already, in your former library or in other organizations you have worked with? You may wish to create a more-or-less formal marketing plan that talks about your services, your customers, and your strategies, setting target goals for your new business and outlining the marketing efforts you will take to achieve these. Setting measurable goals helps you focus your marketing strategies; write these down and refer to them frequently. Your specific strategies will depend on your type of business and its natural market.

Entrepreneurship

Entrepreneurs must take a more deliberate and strategic approach to building their businesses than those who choose the kind of blended careers outlined in Chapter 4. These types of businesses combine less well with a full-time job, or even a part-time job; your availability during regular business hours and your commitment to your clients are key. When running your own business, be sure to factor in the time you must spend doing "nonbillable" work, from marketing to bookkeeping to buying office supplies to just plain keeping up with the field.

An entrepreneur's mindset necessarily differs from that of someone working in a nonprofit or governmental environment. If you are an academic, public, or school librarian, it can be difficult to make this switch, to realize that your activities now are targeted toward making a profit, and that a big chunk of your time will be taken up in marketing yourself. The lack of an inherent structure to your workday can also be difficult to get used to—especially for librarians! As your own boss, you need to motivate and manage yourself. You will need to impose your own order on your work life and develop exceptional time-management skills. As Cindy Mediavilla, lecturer, UCLA, Library Programs Consultant, California State Library, and freelance consultant/trainer, explains, you "must be highly self-motivated, especially if working at home. It's very easy to get distracted by everyday tasks, like doing laundry, paying bills, etc. Working at home should be treated just like going to the office, only you don't have to waste two hours in the morning deciding what to wear and fighting traffic!"

In order to succeed, entrepreneurs must also be willing to take risks and have a high comfort level with change. This differs from the less-than-risky daily life of many librarians, so if you picked the field because of its perceived stability, you need to do a realistic self-evaluation to see if entrepreneurship truly fits your personality and preferences, or if you might do better seeking employment in an existing company.

Transferable skills and qualities for entrepreneurs vary depending on the direction you decide to take your business, but can include:

- Analysis

- Budgeting

- Decision making

- Management

- Marketing

- Multitasking

- Negotiation

- Problem solving

- Self-motivation

When launching your business or expanding it into a full-time venture, you may also need to raise funds. Info brokers, for example, will need access to subscription databases that can cost thousands per year. Any business today will need high-speed Internet access, phone, fax, and other investments in technology. See whether you can realistically self-fund your venture, or whether you will need to seek outside funding.

Judy Koren, self-employed information specialist, Haifa, Israel, sums up these necessary entrepreneurial qualities: "If you want to run your own business, you have to have a totally unjustified belief in your own abilities—don't let the world get you down, because there will always be people who tell you that you can't do it, it won't work, etc. You also need the ability to live with uncertainty. You never know more than a month in advance how much money will be coming in. You need faith that those orders will arrive, the clients will return, etc. I think this is the main reason why people return to employment after having been self-employed."

It Chose Me

I was working in a solo corporate library for a company I can only describe as information averse and brain dead. They pitted cost centers against each other, so no one wanted to cooperate and share information, nor did anyone want to pay for information—after all, "it's all on the Internet for free." I got tired of fighting this, being bored at work (since fewer people were using the library), and being moved from department to department (since no one wanted to pay for my overhead). So, I walked out. I didn't know what I was going to do next.

My first book, *The SOLO Librarian's Sourcebook*, had just been published. After some personal issues were taken care of, I received a call from Guy St. Clair asking if I wanted to buy his newsletter, *The One-Person Library: A Newsletter for Librarians and Management*. I said yes and started as editor/publisher in May 1998. Obviously, I didn't choose it, it chose me. But it was something I knew I could do—writing comes easily to me and I was vitally interested in helping and promoting solo librarians, having been the first chair of the SOLO Librarian's Division of SLA.

My career has encompassed three areas:

1. *Editor/publisher* – I choose the issue theme, write or collect articles (many come from lists and blog posts), make it all fit into 12 pages, manage a subscription database, and handle renewals—*every* month.

2. *Teacher/speaker* – St. Clair offered to sell me his OPL Management workshop, but I figured I could develop my own. And I did, plus two others: Management Strategies for One-Person Librarians; Time Management, Planning, and Prioritization; and The Visible Librarian: Marketing

and Advocacy. Over the years I have done 50+ workshops around the world (England, Spain, Barcelona,
South Africa, Australia, New Zealand, USA, Canada) as
well as at SLA conferences, and have given short
speeches to SLA groups (and others) for which I do not
charge.

3. *Writer* – In addition to my newsletter, I've written articles for *Searcher, American Libraries, AALL Spectrum,
ALA TechSource,* various Web sites, and other newslet-
ters. There have been six more books: *The OPL
Sourcebook* (2nd ed. of *SOLO Sourcebook*); *Time
Management, Planning and Prioritization for
Librarians; The Visible Librarian: Asserting Your Value
with Marketing and Advocacy; The New OPL Sourcebook*
(3rd ed.); *The Essential OPL* (selections from the
newsletter); and the latest, *Out Front with Stephen
Abram* (a collection of his writings).

There is no such thing as a typical day; I do what needs to
be done. I spend a lot of time online, checking email and
blogs, blogging on "OPL Plus (not just for OPLs any more)"
(opls.blogspot.com), and investigating new resources. I save
good discussions from electronic lists for future articles. I
email to get permissions from everyone I quote in the
newsletter (I almost got sued once for not getting permission). If I'm working on a book, I'll spend a lot of time
researching or writing. I read the professional literature. I
belong to 10 library associations around the world (SLA,
MLA, AALL, CLA, CILIP, ALIA, LIANZA, LIASA, and a couple
of smaller groups), and read their publications plus any
books I can find on subjects of interest to my customers.
This is a joy; I never had time to read this stuff when I was
"working." And there's the office work involved in running a

business: receiving checks, updating the subscriber database, paying bills, updating software, getting hardware updated/fixed.

Many of the skills/knowledge I use on the job were *not* taught in library school: time management, how to start and run a small business, marketing (and by that I mean more than PR or publicity—assessing your product and services and the competition, and making a marketing plan). Since I'd worked mostly in the corporate world and as a solo, I knew more than many librarians about competition and proving your value, so I just had to learn more about it and how to apply it to libraries. Much of the stuff I read and use in my work is *not* from the library literature, but from business, management, PR, etc.

If you want to do it, do it! Life is too short to do something you don't love. But look before you leap. How will you pay your bills until you get established? (A spouse/partner working for a "real" company helps.) What about insurance (health, liability, physical contents)? Do you have the infrastructure (computer, cable modem, place to work, personal/professional network)? Would I do this again? In a heartbeat! What's next? I plan to "retire" in about 2 years—dunno what I'll do then, but it's time for something new.

Judith Siess is President, Information Bridges International, Inc., Cleveland, OH.

Running a Research Business/ Becoming an Info Broker

One of the most relevant ways to strike out on your own is to put your research and information skills to work as an info broker, whether you call yourself an independent information professional (IIP), an information entrepreneur, an info broker, or a research business. While this section introduces the idea of becoming an info broker, you can find titles that go into much more depth in Appendix D at the end of this book, including Mary Ellen Bates' excellent *Building & Running a Successful Research Business* (ITI, 2003). You may also wish to investigate one or more of the titles in ITI's Super Searchers series (books.infotoday.com/ books/index.shtml#sss) for more on providing research services in specific subject areas. Becoming an info broker can be a fantastic option for both MLS holders and non-MLS holders with a library or research background, who can put their research and analysis skills to work for organizations less concerned about specific degrees than about the quality of their work.

So, what do busy info brokers do all day? At its most basic, information brokering involves providing information services such as customized fee-based research, which is often more in-depth and requires more analysis than the questions one might encounter at a busy public or academic reference desk. Many info brokers do corporate research, often starting out by doing contract work for a previous employer or by specializing in the same area of research as in their current job, while some provide contract services to libraries or to individuals. They use multiple resources to find answers, from the invisible Web to fee-based services to government databases and public records to telephone research.

While information brokers' work in many ways resembles that of reference librarians, there are a number of important differences. Info brokers, for example, often specialize in one or more subject areas, offering specific expertise rather than the general assistance one finds at most public and academic library reference desks. These specialties can include subject knowledge such as medical expertise, skills in patent and trademark searching, or an industry-specific background. As an info broker you can choose to market yourself to a broader range of potential clients rather than specializing, but this will require additional marketing skills and can dilute your brand recognition. Beyond providing basic answers and facts, information brokers also often write detailed reports analyzing the research they have undertaken and discussing the meaning and implications of the results. This can be a good path to take if you enjoy and are skilled at writing and analysis, not just research; a good info broker needs to provide added value to clients above and beyond what they might get by calling their local library.

While some info brokers form partnerships with others, they most often work as solo professionals. One of your biggest obstacles may be the lack of coworkers to serve as sounding boards for your ideas, to pick up some of the slack—or to make any of the decisions for you! This is one reason why healthy networks are so important for a solo professional. If you're a people person and need regular in-person contact with others to energize you and keep you focused, you had better work out ways to build this contact into your life before jumping into a solo career. Think about whether virtual relationships will fill the "water-cooler" gap for you; think about ways to retain relationships with your current colleagues; think about scheduling regular lunches or joining networking groups; continue to attend relevant conferences and maintain your involvement in local professional organizations. Your networks with other independent professionals can be invaluable, and you can also subcontract work to other info pros in your network who specialize in different areas, while receiving similar opportunities from them.

Working as an info broker can be difficult to balance with your personal life, due to the often-short deadlines and irregular workflow. If a large, well-paying project comes up, it needs to take precedence over any personal activities you may have planned. If multiple projects appear simultaneously, it's hard to say no. If you are choosing to leave library work in part to build more balance into your life, a career as an info broker may not be optimal.

However, as an information entrepreneur, you can enjoy the free-dom of working for yourself—sans meetings, committees, bureau-cracy, apathetic coworkers, foot-dragging administrators, and all the other frustrations often inherent to library work.

To strike out on your own as an info broker, research skills alone are not enough; marketing skills are at least as important, if not more so. Especially at first, you will need to devote a great deal of time to building up your business and making a name for yourself, not to mention actually doing the work! Ways to market yourself include networking at professional and local events, getting involved with associations and organizations, creating an effective online presence for your business, and getting listed in consultant registries and specialized directories. IIPs also often create and give workshops or presentations and write for industry publica-tions, both to tap into an additional source of income and to help increase their name recognition in their target market.

Over time, you will reduce the amount of marketing you need to do by building ongoing relationships with your clients; repeat cus-tomers can be the lifeblood of your business. In the long run, it costs you much more to find a new customer than to retain a good one. Working with multiple repeat clients also offers you some sta-bility: Even if you lose one, you have additional streams of income from the others.

Many researchers start small, either doing research on the side for current contacts or seeking opportunities online. Realize that sites like craigslist (www.craigslist.org), while containing a number of ads for freelance researchers, also tend to drive prices down—their very popularity leads to too much competition, and people tend to choose cheap over quality. In order to make any money in the field and to establish yourself as a professional, you need to market yourself as an information *professional*. (For more on doing research on the side, see Chapter 3.) Most IIPs find it hard to balance their independent work with a day job, often finding that they need to make the full-time leap to have the time and energy to be successful. This leap is easiest if you start out with at least one regular client, most often a former employer. Market yourself first to your existing network.

One of your marketing tools can be the cost savings and value-added services you can provide; tout the high return on investment from using your services. Companies use info brokers to reduce their costs—using an outside source keeps them from needing to hire a full-time research analyst or other specialist. Realize, though, that their reduced costs don't translate into the need for you to reduce your fees. The company's savings on benefits, full-time salaries, and other expenditures make independent information specialists a relative bargain even at a living wage.

When setting your fees, think about whether you wish to bill by the hour or by the project. Most info brokers recommend charging per project. To do so effectively, you'll need to develop skills in estimating how long a given project is likely to take, and then come up with your private hourly rate. Some companies may be more comfortable with an hourly rate, while others may give you a "do not exceed" budget, asking you to report your findings after reaching that dollar amount so it can be determined whether to take the project further. Mary Ellen Bates' *Building & Running a Successful Research Business* contains a very useful chapter on setting rates and fees; be sure to read her recommendations and caveats before setting yours. Also realize that being an info broker is not like traditional reference librarianship, where you can keep digging for an answer indefinitely. You will need to limit yourself to researching only as long as your client will pay you. This is again part of valuing your own time and skills: Don't give them away.

Successful info brokers get to duplicate much of what's fun about reference librarianship, but can avoid many of the headaches inherent in public service. If you enjoy research, finding things out, and analyzing information, if you have an entrepreneurial spirit and a strong network, this may be the path for you. The initial steps, though, have much in common with the reference desk— starting with a successful reference interview to get to the heart of what your client is really looking for.

Transferable skills and personal qualities for info brokers include:

- Analysis

- Commitment to lifelong learning

- Communication, especially online

- Entrepreneurial outlook

- Marketing

- Research

- Writing

Think about where your own strengths lie.

Freedom and Impact

While completing the MLIS program at University of Denver, I attended the six-week Publishing Institute. I had previously worked for the *Denver Magazine*, and loved publishing because it was about creating information. I found I was much more interested in finding information, creating information, or "putting it in play," than in organizing and managing it. The traditionally reactive role of librarianship—i.e., waiting for someone to come in and ask for information— didn't suit me; I was much more interested in actively finding ways and opportunities to get information into people's hands so they could use it to accomplish something. So my various engagements as an information professional have involved advising, building, and creating, doing activities where information was in an outreach, rather than a passive, role.

My career is based on the key resource of information, and how people can use it to improve or change their lives, whether at the individual, organization, or community level. I have found myself using my LIS-based research skills in almost every project I've worked on. So I would say the ability to find, manage, evaluate, synthesize, summarize, and organize information has been central to almost everything I do.

I have worked in publishing as a managing and acquisitions editor; worked as an executive information advisor for a cable telecommunications CEO; worked as a special librarian for a cultural institution; run an MLIS program on an interim basis; designed and created the first virtual library for online students and then launched a profitable business based on that product; ghostwritten several books as well as writing several under my own name; and worked as an independent doing information projects, research, and content creation for numerous nonprofit and for-profit organizations. In addition, I created and have now taught for nearly 10 years a course on alternative career paths for LIS students and professionals.

In broad strokes, I work with information on behalf of clients in order to help them attain some sort of business or organizational goal. This work could be research, writing, online content creation, creating information-management processes and procedures, or helping a client figure out ways to use information content and resources as strategic assets for the organization. For example, I might be helping a nonprofit create and post on its Web site useful information for its members, the media, potential donors, etc. Goals might be to help extend the reach of educational outreach, increase membership, build visibility as a topic authority with the media, build credibility with potential donors as thought-leaders in the field, etc. The first step is to identify the strategic goals, then determine the most effective way to use information resources to execute against those targets. In addition, I work with students, former students, and colleagues to help them determine and then successfully pursue their career goals.

My career offers me both freedom and impact:

- *Freedom* – Although I am always willing to be an employee if it's the only way I can have an opportunity to work on a project that really intrigues me (such as when I led the creation of the Jones eglobal virtual library for Jones International), my ongoing preference is to have the freedom to do whatever work engages me. Working as an independent allows me a breathtaking level of diversity in the projects I work on, and also offers an ongoing opportunity to learn new things, meet new people, and chart new paths.
- *Impact* – I love having the opportunity to create or contribute to new solutions that have a positive impact on people or organizations or communities. Because I'm an independent, I'm free to step up and contribute my information skills wherever I see a need or an opportunity. I believe passionately that information is the world's most powerful change agent, but only if we find ways to "get it in play." My career choices have been around that goal.

My undergraduate degree was in English, so I already had pretty good writing skills, which I need daily. But more than anything, what I needed was to embrace an attitude that my skills and knowledge were valuable, important, and should be respected.

One of my first jobs after grad school was working as the personal information advisor to the CEO of a large cable telecommunications company. I had to be confident in my knowledge and judgment, because he was relying on me to provide strategic information to the organization. If I had come across as anything less than confident, he would have had no respect for my abilities. I couldn't have done my job if I had been hesitant, passive, or unwilling to "own" my recommendations. I quickly understood the "fake it until you make it" concept. In other words, you fake the level of confidence you need until you get to the point where you finally feel it. And, you get to *that* point by being good at your job over and over again, and then looking back and finally acknowledging "damn, I *AM* good!" And it's important to note, that's not arrogance, it's competence.

I've also had to get over the "I don't know how to do this, so I'd better not accept the assignment because I might fail" response. I've often been asked to do something that seemed incredibly cool, so in a fit of enthusiasm I've agreed to take the work on. Then, at a later, more rational moment (usually as I'm lying awake at three in the morning), I go through the *"what was I thinking?"* response, as I realize I have no clue what I'm doing. This used to lead to major anxiety (okay, it still does), but then I started watching how men handled these types of situations. They just took it for granted that they were so amazingly capable, *of course* they would be wildly successful at whatever they were taking on. Now, these guys weren't any smarter than I was, they just had this breathtaking assumption of success—that they would be able to figure out whatever they needed to complete the assignment.

So I decided to start making the same assumptions. And so far, it's worked.

If you are considering a similar path:

1. Consider your skills in the broadest possible context. How many ways can you contribute? How many different organizations can use your skills?

2. Take a long-term view of your career, and focus on what you want to achieve with every project (or job) you work on. What do you want to learn? What new goal do you want to achieve? What people do you want to develop relationships with?

3. Understand that we are all self-employed. Things change—in your work, in your personal life, in who you are and what brings you joy—over the course of your career. By understanding, accepting, and preparing for that fact, you are less likely to be devastated when those changes happen.

4. Take a leadership role in developing your career. This will allow you to contribute at your highest level, while also creating opportunities for you to help others do the same.

Kim Dority is Information Strategist and President, G. K. Dority & Associates, Inc., Denver, CO.

Whether you call yourself an info broker, a researcher, or an independent information professional, you will benefit from having a strong network of contacts to draw on and a strong understanding of the ins and outs of the field. Resources and associations for independent information workers include:

- Association of Independent Information Professionals (AIIP), www.aiip.org (AIIP also provides a mentoring program for new members, www.aiip.org/aboutAIIP/aiipmentor.html)

- Frequently Asked Questions About Information Brokering, www.marketingbase.com/faqs.html

- Independent Librarians Exchange (ILEX), www.ala.org/ala/ascla/asclaourassoc/asclasections/ilex/ilex.cfm

- Info-Entrepreneurship, www.batesinfo.com/info-brokering.html

- *ONLINE*, www.infotoday.com/online

- Online Insider, www.onlineinsider.net

- Resources for Independent Careers, www.rethinking informationwork.com/Independent%20Careers.html

If you are interested in getting started in the field, think about asking an existing IIP if you can take on some contract work or shadow him or her for a day. You can also offer your services on a volunteer basis to some local organizations or to other IIPs in order to build up a portfolio of work to show to future clients.

Becoming a Vendor

While Chapter 2 discussed the idea of working for an existing vendor, you can also explore the possibility of striking out on your own to provide a needed service to libraries. Since libraries are such a niche market, it's often more important to have a knowledge of their specific needs and outlook than to have knowledge of specific technologies or products. Technical knowledge can be acquired; relationships take time to build.

If you intend to become a vendor, first think about what potential niche your new company could fill. Think about *why* and *how*.

What services or products do you wish your current vendors provided? Is there a product that you or your colleagues have looked for, yet been unable to find? What could you provide more cost effectively than the big guys? What are the "pain points" in libraries' relationships with their existing vendors, and how could you resolve these? What value could you add to existing products or services? How would you market yourself to libraries and librarians?

Next, consider factors such as startup costs. Will you need equipment? Programmers? Office space? Will you need to travel to conferences and lease booth space in exhibit halls? How much will all this run you? How will you fund your new venture? Do you have potential customers already lined up?

A good example of a successful librarian-created vendor venture is Serials Solutions, Inc., which grew from a basement operation to a profitable company and was acquired by ProQuest in 2004. The company was created in 2000 by reference librarian Peter McCracken, growing out of his frustration at the difficulty of locating and managing constantly changing eresources. Think about your own frustration points at work, or what you've heard librarians complain about at conferences. How could your new company solve these issues?

Transferable skills, experience, and qualities for librarians-turned-vendors include:

- Computer programming
- Knowledge of the library market
- Marketing
- Networks and relationships
- Sales
- Technical

Librarians turned vendors have a leg up on the competition in their intimate knowledge of and connections with the library market. As in any entrepreneurial venture, draw on your existing relationships and skills for the best chance of success.

Endnotes

1. Jessamyn West, introduction to Priscilla K. Shontz and Richard A. Murray, eds., *A Day in the Life: Career Options in Library and Information Science,* Westport, CT: Libraries Unlimited, 2007: xix.
2. Sarah and Paul Edwards, *Secrets of Self-Employment: Surviving and Thriving on the Ups and Downs of Being Your Own Boss,* New York: Putnam, 1991, 1996: 52.
3. Ruth I. Gordon, "On Behalf of Children," in Betty-Carol Sellen, ed., *What Else You Can Do with a Library Degree: Career Options for the 90s and Beyond,* New York: Neal-Schuman, 1997: 29.

Chapter 6

Information Work

It is that ability to make connections—to understand context and thrive in complexity—that underpins success in the commercial world, for organizations and for individuals. That ability gives an information professional the platform they need to maximize their skills in the commercial world and to take new opportunities.[1]

As organizations recognize the importance of managing and making accessible ever-increasing quantities of information, information professionals' skills, both in managing information and in training end-users to find and use that information, become ever more crucial. Librarians bring their expertise to information-related fields as varied as competitive intelligence (CI), knowledge management (KM), data mining, records information management (RIM), project management, fundraising, prospect research, search, and market research. Regardless of their specific title and duties, each of these professionals in some way uses or manages information to help an organization reach its strategic goals.

When we fail to consider entering these and other related fields, on the assumption that they range too far from traditional librarianship, we cede the emerging information landscape to noninformation professionals, and we fail to best utilize our skills and position our profession for the new economy. Furthermore, in an era of corporate downsizing, info pros who can disassociate themselves from the library as a separate entity and integrate themselves into positions of strategic importance throughout their organizations may better be able to weather inevitable storms and position themselves to take advantage of inevitable changes. Those who show an ability and willingness to move into different roles both prove their value to their companies and keep their skills fresh.

When searching for jobs working with information, realize that many positions with day-to-day duties that incorporate much of what we think of as library work might be viewed by companies as something else entirely. Jobs that facilitate the free flow of information or involve organizing information within a company or governmental entity can be carried out by a degreed librarian or someone with an IS degree, but are often filled by someone with a background in another subject entirely. Expand your job search to include relevant titles and terminology such as:

- Analyst
- Competitive intelligence
- Content manager
- Data mining
- Data modeler
- Document management
- Information architect
- Information manager
- Knowledge manager
- Knowledge officer
- Market researcher
- Ontologist
- Project manager
- Records manager

- Researcher

- RIM (Records/Information Management)

- Strategic planning

- Taxonomist

Just a few of these fields will be discussed in the following sections; find more on searching for nontraditional positions in Appendix A. As one survey respondent suggests, "A lot of librarians get themselves into ruts; an example would be catalogers. Keep yourself diversified; think outside your box. Our skills are transferable to project management, education, competitive and business intelligence searching ... I could go on and on."

Some of these information-related jobs seem more "nontraditional" than others: Some librarians might see them all as nontraditional, while others might not consider any of them to be outside the scope of librarianship. It all depends on how we define our field and draw our own boundaries. The extent to which a position is nontraditional often lies in the eye of the beholder, in the ways in which companies view and classify various positions. Some may use industry- or company-specific terminology not even included in the preceding list, so take time to research the way information work is classified in your targeted organization(s) or field. In general, info pros in these types of positions command better salaries than librarians working in traditional roles in traditional organizations—and both your salary and the way in which you are regarded can hinge on how the company defines your role.

Realize also that many of these related specialties, while drawing on traditional library and information skills, do require further expansion of your skills and knowledge base. As Abell and Wingar point out: "The traditional career path for LIS professionals in the commercial sector remains. Undoubtedly there is a growing requirement for core information skills—for the ability to research, code, and organize information, to manage information

Not Nontraditional?

I worked for about 15 years in the media field in a production capacity, where job security is rare and job searching a constant. Regardless of my title, I always seemed to be tagged as the person to create and manage databases and to compile and share information. Pre-library school, I was working at Yahoo! on an online financial news program, which went away after two and a half years in 2003. The company gave us free career counseling when they let us go, and I realized I might make a good librarian—so I went and got my MLS.

I'm not sure if I qualify as nontraditional, unless you consider corporate libraries to be so. I work in what is essentially a music library at an Internet company. We have physical assets (CDs and music in many different video formats), but the bulk of our collection is increasingly digital, as more and more of the music we sell is electronically fed to us directly from the labels. There is no reference desk, although we do handle user feedback from customers and internal Yahoos. Most of the work we do is data rights management; I do a lot of QA [quality assurance] comparing our services to those of the competition. I train and oversee contractors who do a lot of data entry, maintain the data entry guidelines, and am involved in data cleansing projects.

I love special libraries, and during school I always imagined I'd get a job in a news library. Unfortunately, I live in California, and all the good news library jobs are on the east coast. The best thing about my career is I'm doing what I like to do (organizing information), and I hope that my experience here will transfer to other special libraries. I work with three other MLS librarians; we call where we work the music library. But I don't know that I could walk into a random public library and immediately find everything I'm looking for much faster than the average civilian.

An education focused on how to organize information is valuable at work, where we deal with tons of data. Nonlibrarians in this environment tend to focus more on the surface level, whereas we stress the importance of creating and sticking to structure and hierarchy. Some other companies in this space operate without data entry standards or guidelines, and you just know they don't hire librarians. Studying DRM in class was definitely different from hands-on day-to-day experience, although having a familiarity with some of the terminology was helpful. Having a background in old media is helpful in much the same way; some of my colleagues who have only ever worked in new media aren't familiar with obsolete media formats or broadcasting production terms that we occasionally come across.

If interested in a similar career, start networking early, get involved with SLA as a student, and see as much as you can of what's out there as far as different libraries. Knowing you're not interested in traditional libraries (children, academic, or public) as a student gives you a great advantage, as you can tailor each assignment to special libraries, thus parlaying them into networking opportunities.

Emi Y. Bevacqua is Content Specialist, Yahoo!, Santa Monica, CA.

supply, and to transfer key skills to other people. But the growth is in new careers—in roles that are not conveniently labeled 'information or library specialists.'"[2] Those who create successful synergy among multiple roles and who extend their work and their influence outside of the "library" will find success.

An Interview with Deborah Schwarz, President and CEO, Library Associates Companies (LAC), Los Angeles, CA

Of the information professional placements you do each year, about what percent would you say are into nontraditional positions? Can you talk a little bit about some of the typical nontraditional positions your agency fills?

Probably about 40 percent are nontraditional in the sense that they are positions requiring "library" skills but are not in a library. For example, managing content for an ecommerce organization's Intranet; providing consultation on taxonomy and metatagging for a publishing company's internal clients; managing a company's information management workflow when they reorganize from private work sites to a global/ flexible environment; and other similar types of jobs. We see the trend increasingly toward nontraditional positions for information professionals, but the gaps for us as recruiters are that many candidates are not interested in positions requiring sales, management, and consultation in combination with "library skills," and many companies don't know that they could use a librarian for the job. We are always educating clients and persuading candidates to look at their experience and skill sets from a different angle.

What kind of personal qualities and transferable skills are most useful in these types of careers?

A successful information professional who may want to work outside of the library will need to have:

- Excellent communication skills – Not only writing a decent email, but the ability to get up in front of a group and present.

- Training and teaching skills – As more and more users move into a self-serve environment, they need greater training and orientation on how to conduct efficient searches.
- Knowing what the best sources and content are and how to find them, as more and more resources proliferate.
- Budgeting and accounting and an understanding of the organization's P&L; the ability to read license agreements and negotiate contracts for content.
- Management – Knowing how to effectively supervise, manage, mentor, and train others are key skills, as well as having the ability to manage a project—knowing how to use project management software, design and implement a project schedule, etc.

How can info pros best prepare themselves for changes in information work?

Stay on top of your reading and take courses in the appropriate areas. Learn how to use Excel or how to read a financial report, take public speaking courses, learn as much as possible about the field or industry you support, and stay on top of that industry. Get involved in relevant professional organizations outside of the library field. I also think it is important for those who are successful to give back to those who are entering the field—teach at the library school, get on an advisory board.

When it comes to information-focused jobs within organizations, transferable skills and traits for librarians and info pros include both those learned in school and those acquired on the job. These can include both personal and technical skills, as well as personal qualities and talents, such as:

- Analysis

- Communication

- Decision making

- IT skills

- Management

- Organizational skills

- Problem solving

- Project management

- People skills

- Research

- Teamwork

- Technology training

Be ready to make your case—companies may not automatically think of someone with an MLS or library background for many information-related positions and may not classify these as "librarian" work. Your job here is to make prospective employers see the importance and relevance of your skills (find more on this in Appendix A).

Sharon Srodin emphasizes that "… organizations need professionals with industry knowledge who possess core technical skills as well as research and analytical capabilities. Savvy librarians looking to break out of the traditional mold can capitalize on this situation and land interesting, challenging jobs far removed from the traditional information center."[3] You can also investigate these types of careers by attending programs at conferences such as Special Libraries Association (SLA) Annual or by pursuing subject-specific coursework. Anyone interested in doing information work in a corporate environment, whether as a traditional "librarian" or in an alternative role, should investigate SLA (www.sla.org), which offers specialized divisions, programs, and other support and resources for nontraditional info pros. Use SLA's resources and networks to find information on various specialties and to connect with others working in these fields.

If you are already working as a corporate librarian, be alert to the possibility of expanding your role and of moving into a new, nonlibrarian position within your organization. Many companies favor internal candidates, and if you have proven yourself in your current position you can easily make the case as to how your skills transfer to a new role. If you are moving to a corporate information role from a public, academic, or school library, you will need to adjust to working in a corporate environment, with its different focus and priorities. As one survey respondent suggests, "Consider why you entered the library profession. The corporate world has different objectives than the library world. It can offer challenges, opportunities, and larger salaries, but you need to be ready to contribute to the bottom line. If your passion is front line reference, then the corporate world probably is not for you—because the focus is different."

The following sections outline just a few of the most common nontraditional information-related roles librarians tend to fill. Also explore the option of doing librarian-type work in unusual or interesting environments. Google, for instance, sometimes advertises for MLIS-holders to fill positions such as *content analyst* and *library collections specialist* for the Google Book Search project. Combining IT and librarianship, such positions often require both an MLIS and a background or undergraduate degree in computer science. (For more on working in IT in general, see Chapter 8, Working in IT Outside of Libraries.)

Fundraising, Grant Writing, and Prospect Research

One easy jump for information professionals is into the field of fundraising, grant writing, or prospect research. When working in prospect research, for example, rather than researching particular topics, you are researching individuals: their wealth, propensity to give, interests, and history of contributions. Prospect researchers prepare profiles and supply information to their institution's fundraisers, giving them the background they need to successfully ask for donations. Just as in public and academic libraries, this work supports the organization's larger mission and is carried out in service to the community, although the community and your clients may be defined much differently. Fundraising and grant writing for any entity will also resemble fundraising and grant writing in libraries—though perhaps on a larger scale. As fundraiser, you need to make effective use of information, and you may also do your own research. For grant writing, your research skills are patently useful. You might have written grants at your institution and have direct experience, and you can also use your skills in analyzing data and locating opportunities.

In each of these fields, you specifically use the same types of research skills you would as a librarian. As Merissa Enterline, Coordinator of Prospect Research, Middlebury College, Middlebury, VT, says: "I see myself as a research librarian for my fundraising team. If they need something, I find it. My advanced search skills, knowledge of trustworthy sites, and my ability to pick facts out of the vast sea of the Internet are things that I would needas a librarian or a researcher." Another survey respondent involved in freelance development/fundraising research explains: "Basically this field prepares profiles of individuals, corporations,

Making a Difference

Upon graduating in 2002, I was pretty certain that I wanted to work in a special library, as opposed to a public or academic library. My company, KCI (Ketchum Canada Inc.), was offering an entry-level position with the potential to open new doors and prepare me for more senior positions.

A job in prospect research stood out, as I realized that it gave me the opportunity to help make a difference in the world. KCI is a fundraising consulting firm specializing in custom solutions for extraordinary organizations. At KCI, I am in charge of our nonprofit clients in western Canada (Alberta, Saskatchewan, and British Columbia). My work consists of:

- Creating profiles of individuals, corporations, and foundations for our consultants to use on their campaigns
- Working on various special projects, such as prospect identification, strategic planning research, and recruiting projects
- Monitoring our student research assistants (library students) who help us input data and work on special projects
- Tracking government funding announcements from across Canada, and various other press releases related to my region
- Working on *Research Update*, our publication that highlights philanthropic activity in Canada
- Creating and maintaining a knowledge management program
- Leading various training sessions on prospect research
- Presenting on prospect research at conferences

Before I applied for a prospect research position, I didn't even know that the field existed. They may have mentioned it during my MLIS program, but if they did, it was buried underneath all the talk of public and academic libraries. Concepts that I learned in school, such as organization and business research, certainly apply to my job as a prospect researcher, along with Internet searching and database searching abilities. Some transferable skills include:

- Online search skills for newspaper searches (databases) and Google. (I couldn't do my job without Google, and knowing how to use it properly is worth its weight in gold!)
- My knowledge management/record management skills, as I'm in charge of implementing this program for my company.
- Skills that I learned in my competitive intelligence class, such as how to research corporations.
- Skills I learned in management classes, such as how to budget and manage resources and people.
- Experience from doing various presentations in library school, which helped me hone my presentation skills and helped me with training and presenting in my field.

Since I started my job directly after receiving my degree, I wasn't that experienced with business-style writing. I ended up taking a business writing class to help me use less of an essay-writing style, and one more suited to business. Also, I have attended some special library events in Toronto, and am on the board of APRA (Association for Professional Researchers for Advancement) Canada (www.apracanada. ca), where the majority of members are librarians working in the prospect research field.

I most enjoy the people—fundraisers are excellent people to work with, as they are passionate about what they do and the organizations they are working with. Also, the research is exciting! Every day, I have something completely different to tackle, from finding information on a particular company to researching what special events occur in my city. I have to think creatively with each project; there is never a dull day.

As in most jobs, there are the occasional tight deadlines, and the research can be time consuming—which means that at times there is a high level of stress. Also, some projects can get bumped at the last second for last-minute client requests. As for the difference between working in a public library versus a special library, I do miss working with patrons! I always enjoyed working with people who were passionate about books and learning.

I do appreciate the salary, as well as having more and different ways to advance in the company—I could eventually become a Manager or a Vice President of Research.

Shannon Rafferty is Consultant, Research Services, KCI (Ketchum Canada Inc.; www.kciphilanthropy.com), Toronto, Ontario, Canada.

and foundations for front-line fundraisers who use the information to formulate a solicitation—the saying in the field is finding the right donor for the right project for the right gift at the right time. The field varies from people with PhDs to some folks without any undergraduate degree. Several MLIS/MLS folks are here though, as it really suits our skill set. I think this should be an alternative for other librarians."

Those wanting to remain even closer to their library roots can look into fundraising/grant writing positions in LIS schools (see

Chapter 2, Organizations Serving Libraries and Librarians) or libraries (see Chapter 9, Nontraditional Roles, Traditional Institutions). Here, again, your library background and insider knowledge will be a remarkable asset in landing and succeeding in your new position. You may be responsible both for locating and applying for grants and for assisting others with their proposals. Transferable skills, background, and strengths here include:

- Analysis

- Fundraising experience

- Grant writing experience

- Online searching

- Presenting

- Research skills

- Written and verbal communication skills

Working as a fundraiser, grant writer, or prospect researcher carries with it the knowledge that you are working to do good, which can be important if you entered library work specifically to make a difference in your community. Another benefit, especially if you work for a consulting firm, is that you will have the opportunity to research a wide variety of companies, people, and fields— again, a great idea for the Renaissance person. Resources for those in these fields include:

- Association of Fundraising Professionals (AFP), www.afpnet.org

- Association of Professional Researchers for Advancement (APRA), www.aprahome.org

- Foundation Directory Online, www.fconline.fdncenter.org

As with any change of career, begin networking and making contacts in your new field for the best chance of success.

Competitive Intelligence (CI)

The art of competitive intelligence (CI) involves using your research and analytical skills to gather and analyze relevant information—including hidden information—about the competitive environment that affects an organization. This information is then used to help the company make informed decisions regarding strategic directions. Beyond sheer research, CI requires the ability to provide value-added analysis—and to provide both factual information and analysis on a timely basis. The Society of Competitive Intelligence Professionals (SCIP; www.scip.org) defines competitive intelligence as "the legal and ethical collection and analysis of information regarding the capabilities, vulnerabilities, and intentions of business competitors."

Transferable skills and qualities for competitive intelligence professionals include:

- Analytical skills
- Ethical foundation
- Evaluation of information
- Research skills

Beyond SCIP, which offers two bimonthly publications, an enewsletter, and other resources for those moving into the field of CI, check out SLA's Competitive Intelligence Division (units.sla. org/division/dci/cihome.htm). Get members-only access to its discussion list and community of practice, read its bulletin, and attend its conference programs. Members can also consider earning a CI certificate from SLA (www.sla.org/CIcertificates, members only).

To avoid ethical conflicts, competitive intelligence work is sometimes outsourced to CI firms or IIPs (independent information professionals; see Chapter 5). You can investigate employment at one of these firms or consider striking out on your own, especially if you have already gained some CI experience in your current organization.

Records Information Management (RIM)

Records management, or records information management, involves the systematic analysis and control of an organization's records (documents), including paper documents, email messages, database content, and Web and other electronic documents. Records managers recognize that every document associated with a company's business activities is a strategic asset. They help companies meet federal record-keeping provisions, organize their records for easy retrieval, and secure critical information.

The principal professional organization for records information managers is ARMA International (www.arma.org). ARMA offers online coursework in the fundamentals of records information management, books and other publications, an annual conference, and other member benefits. Also check out the Institute of Certified Records Managers (ICRM; www.icrm.org), a certifying organization for records information managers.

Records management positions are often listed by staffing agencies that specialize in information-related placements. Start your search by visiting the job search pages at firms like ASRC Management Services (www.asrcms.com) and Library Associates (www.libraryassociates.com/searchjobs.html); search for terms like *records* and *RIM*. You can also search for RIM positions at ARMA International (www.arma.org/careers/index.cfm).

Knowledge Management (KM)

In some cases, information work can be nontraditional more in the sense of its title and location than in the specific functions performed. Knowledge management (KM) recognizes that an organization's knowledge is its most valuable asset, and that effective decision-making requires effective management of that knowledge. KM involves organizing a corporation's knowledge assets and optimizing an environment for collaboration and knowledge sharing, a process that parallels traditional librarianship in many respects. Some of those working in KM see themselves as librarians, even if they are not labeled or seen as such by their institutions. Some see their duties expand beyond traditional library work and wouldn't necessarily define themselves as librarians—again, this depends on the organization, its needs, and where you draw the lines.

Virtual KM

My career is nontraditional in that I work from home for a company with about 85 percent of its employees working virtually. Almost everything is done through email, phone calls, conference calls, a company portal, and instant messaging. I do mostly reference work, but since I am a solo right now, I do anything else that is needed as well, including recommending and purchasing resources and research training. This is probably the perfect job for me—my skill set, experience, and intellectual interest, as well as for my work/life balance.

I love that the company is able to truly employ the best and the brightest in its various categories of expertise, as we are not limited by geography in finding the right people. I like the flexibility of being able to work from home. (I have a small toddler, so just eliminating the commute I used to take to a downtown office enables me to spend more time with him.)

What I like least is the limited opportunity for face-to-face collaboration and the struggles that go with trying to be visible in a virtual environment.

Although I only have a couple of books under my purview that are company property, I am certainly fulfilling the duties of a librarian every day. The art of the reference interview becomes interesting when it is done entirely through email, phone, and instant messaging. Training becomes even more important as well, because everyone is working in different time zones and keeps more flexible hours. I have to make sure that when I am not at my computer or if I have a full plate, there are others who can navigate our resources and find what is needed.

In order to be successful in my career, I did need to figure out how to be visible and how to read people when I only see them once or twice a year. Balance is also a big thing. I work from home, so I have more flexibility, but it also means that my office and computer are always there right next to the work. I do miss the social aspect of being in a library and office setting—but don't miss the commute!

I keep up with the field through SLA events and leadership roles in both my chapter and division. I am chairing the Advertising and Marketing Division and am Secretary of the Minnesota Chapter. I interact with students through SLA and as an adjunct professor in the MLIS program at The College of St. Catherine in St. Paul, MN, and have taught both an elective class, "Issues in Special Libraries," and a core class, "Reference and Online Service."

Deb Rash is Knowledge Manager, Iconoculture, Minneapolis, MN.

Your skill in understanding users' information-seeking behavior and your ability to build cross-departmental bridges are crucial to your success as a knowledge manager. Knowledge managers lack the luxury of locking themselves away in their libraries; they need to involve themselves fully in their organizations (politics and all!) to aid in bringing together disparate strands of knowledge from across the organization.

Resources for knowledge managers include KMWorld (www.kmworld.com) and the related *KMWorld* magazine and annual conference. SLA sponsors a knowledge management division (wiki.sla.org/display/SLAKM) while IFLA offers a KM section (www.ifla.org/VII/s47/index.htm), as do many country-specific special library and information management organizations.

Information Architecture (IA)

Information architecture (IA) brings the principles of design into the digital environment. The Information Architecture Institute (www.iainstitute.org) defines information architecture as "the art and science of organizing and labeling websites, intranets, online communities and software to support usability." IA encompasses components from IT infrastructure to information governance, creating the structural framework that helps get relevant information to users within an organization. Companies that lack (or have dismantled) their traditional libraries often employ information architects to organize and structure their information.

Organizations may employ information architects as such or may seek information architecture skills from those in information management positions. Useful preparation for information architects, beyond a degree in IA, LIS, or IS, includes coursework or experience in usability, information-seeking behavior, HCI (human-computer interaction), interaction design, project management, and information design.

The Information Architecture Institute provides members with benefits such as a job board, mentoring program, educational resources, and an email discussion list. Additional resources for information architects include Jesse James Garrett's online Information Architecture Resources (www.jjg.net/ia), as well as his classic *The Elements of User Experience: User-Centered Design for the Web* (New Riders, 2002). If your LIS interests focus on usability and findability, information architecture may be the path for you.

Search

Search is of obvious and immediate interest to librarians, and search organizations that employ information professionals at various levels end up stronger. Resources for searchers and search creators include:

- Internet Librarian and Internet Librarian International conferences, www.infotoday.com/conferences.shtml
- ResearchBuzz, www.researchbuzz.org
- ResourceShelf, www.resourceshelf.com
- Search Engine University, www.searchengineu.com

While some of these resources focus primarily on search engine optimization or online research techniques, understanding how companies and researchers are taking advantage of search features also helps those in the search industry tweak their engines and implement desired features.

The most obvious transferable skill for those moving to the search industry is cataloging/organization of information. Any technical background and programming skills will also come in handy.

Never Looked Back

Living in the Bay Area in the mid- to late-1990s, I looked around, noticed the rise of search companies, and thought that sounded interesting. When I started my MLIS I assumed I'd be a lifer at SFPL (San Francisco Public Library), where I'd been a paraprofessional for almost 5 years, but things changed when I realized how many other possibilities were available for librarians. Once I started working at search companies I never looked back—and it's been almost 10 years now.

I manage people who specialize in a variety of editorial tasks relating to search quality. That includes relevancy testing (evaluating the quality of search results) and building ontologies or other structures and schemes for classifying Web pages. To people outside the search industry, it is strange that, as a librarian, I work in the search industry. To people in the search industry, it's a no-brainer. Instead of classifying physical objects, I classify Web pages. Instead of conducting in-person reference interviews, I act as a proxy between the searchers and the search engine.

Honestly, though, the skills from my MLIS didn't help much. It's more about how to walk the line between making information both easy to find and correctly organized. I was disappointed with the search engine education in my MLIS program, particularly as San Jose State is in the heart of Silicon Valley. I studied Dialog and a bunch of other electronic databases, which I've never used since graduation; we touched a bit on search engines, but not in any meaningful way. Spidering, crawling, etc., were uncommon terms, at least when I was in school, but these are things I now talk about every day.

I'd like to see MLIS programs with a search engine track. As a hiring manager, I'd hire people like that—like the kinds of tech-savvy librarian-types who are graduating without an MLIS from Berkeley's SIMS program.

The best ways to get a job in the search industry, assuming you don't have connections, are to start a search blog and network on LinkedIn. Most tech recruiters turn to LinkedIn now when looking for candidates. Realize also that MLIS programs prepare people to work in libraries, which generally have a standardized pay scale. When I transferred to the private sector I was totally unprepared for negotiating compensation, and barely even knew what a stock option was. I learned quickly on my own.

I most like the feeling that my work reaches millions of people, particularly when I worked at Yahoo! (2005–2006). I also am thrilled to be one of the non-tech people who interacts with super-smart engineers all day. I least like that because I've taken this path of working in technical companies, I don't always feel I'm involved in the type of creative work I'd like to do, and I miss the family feel of SFPL. I worked in the SF History department with people who'd been there for 20 to 30 years, and you just don't get that in the high-tech industry where people wander between jobs every few years. I do attend Internet Librarian each year, which is a great way to network and meet other techie librarians. I don't miss the limited growth opportunities of being in the civil service.

Chris Fillius is Senior Director of Search Quality, Searchme, Inc., San Francisco, CA.

Traditional Work, Nontraditional Institutions

Is a librarian at Google nontraditional? What about a librarian at *Entertainment Weekly?* In some cases, the work environment is more nontraditional than the actual work performed. Look beyond the traditional library environment to expand your horizons; think about how your nonlibrary skills and background round out your abilities and make you marketable to nontraditional institutions.

Realize, though, that working as a librarian in a nontraditional environment offers its own set of challenges. You may be the only librarian or information worker in your organization, and therefore will lack colleagues to help you out or bounce ideas off of. Your boss may not understand what exactly you do, so you may have to continually market yourself and prove the impact and return on investment of your services. Resources for solo information professionals include Information Bridges International (www.ibi-opl.com) and SLA's Solo Librarians Division (units.sla.org/division/dsol).

Managing Music

As a student in high school and college, I ran the band library. I enjoyed this very much, but never considered it a career option until seeing an advertisement for an opening in the United States Marine Band library. (Although I did not apply at that time, it made me aware of the profession.) After graduate school, I joined an Air Force band in California and volunteered for additional duty responsibilities in the band library, and then later accepted a position on the library staff of the United States Marine Band in Washington, D.C. My career is a natural way to combine my love of both library work and ensemble music.

The primary job of a performance librarian is to make sure the ensemble has the music it needs, when it needs it, to perform a concert. This involves acquiring the music from the music dealer or renting it from the music publisher, preparing it for the musician (marking bowings, correcting errata, fixing bad page turns, etc.), and distributing it to the players. As the source of music for the ensemble, we communicate regularly with organization administrators (music director, personnel manager, stage manager, public relations), as well as with conductors, musicians, and occasionally the public to disseminate information about the repertoire.

Our responsibility is to organize and provide access to the music, much like traditional librarians provide access to their institution's books and materials. Because our libraries are smaller in size and staff than most other libraries, we are responsible for all aspects of library work: acquisitions, cataloging, circulation, and reference. We just deal with nontraditional materials for a specialized audience.

Although performance librarians do not typically catalog their materials using the Anglo-American Cataloguing Rules, we apply many of those concepts to our own cataloging systems. I also use many of the music specific reference sources that I learned in school during the course of my job, as well as the tactics of the reference interview, when I am asked to locate or acquire materials. However, I had to learn the additional responsibilities of preparing music for performance: choosing appropriate editions, identifying and correcting errata (and the fine points of music notation), and formatting printed music for performance. My nonlibrary background as a performing musician was vital to seeing how performing music should be formatted.

Because there is no instructional course for performing librarianship, the best way to learn the work is to apprentice or intern at a professional ensemble library. Alternatively, working as a librarian for a performing ensemble provides hands-on experience and knowledge about the repertoire. Valuable information is also available from the members of the Major Orchestra Librarians' Association (MOLA, the professional organization for performance librarians) and on the MOLA Web site (www.mola-inc.org).

My work in the performance library is very fulfilling. I've had the opportunity to work with professional ensembles of the highest caliber (U.S. Marine Band, Boston Symphony, Boston Pops, New York Philharmonic), and I'm very satisfied with my work.

Russ Girsberger is Ensemble Librarian, The Juilliard School, New York, NY.

Keep an eye on the general library job boards for ads for these types of nontraditional positions, but also frequent industry-specific publications and sites in your fields of interest. Many organizations may not think to advertise on job boards targeting librarians, may not even know that a librarian is who they want, or may get sufficient applications from posting on their own turf. Google, for example, occasionally posts "Librarian Wanted" ads on Google Librarian Central (librariancentral.blogspot.com), assuming that the natural applicant pool for these postings already reads their blog.

While searching, remain open to a broad variety of options. When you envision yourself working in a "library," expand your notion of what that may entail beyond the standard public, academic, school, and corporate categories. Overall, expanding your ideas of what information work entails and looking at *all* of your options allows you more freedom in pursuing the career that's right for you. Once you have seen some of your options, target the skills you need to get there. (Find more on continuing education in Chapter 11, Where To from Here?)

Endnotes

1. Angela Abell and Lucy Wingar, "The Commercial Connection: Realizing the Potential of Information Skills," *Business Information Review* 22:3 (2005): 173.
2. ibid, 176.
3. Sharon Srodin, "Radical Reinvention: Life Beyond the Library," *Searcher* March 2007: 8.

Chapter 7

Working in Very Different Roles

A topic is not a domain with edges. It is how passion focuses itself.[1]

While librarians and information professionals naturally tend to think first about using their skills to succeed in fields that seem in one way or another related to librarianship, or those that draw obviously on info pros' main areas of expertise, you can also think about using your background—or transcending your background—in new and unexpected ways. Perhaps you have found that librarianship just isn't for you, perhaps you long to conquer new frontiers, or perhaps library-related jobs are few and far between in your geographic location. Perhaps an opportunity to use the skills you have gained through a previous career, nonlibrary education, or hobby just happens to come along, or perhaps your volunteer or part-time work in another field turns into a full-time opportunity. Maybe you signed up with a staffing agency that placed you in a position that turned out to be a fantastic fit, or maybe you recently took some time out to reflect and began envisioning yourself in a completely new role.

If nothing else, don't hesitate to make the jump simply because the new career you envision seems so far removed from librarianship. First, your facility with information work comes in handy in *any* career. Second, why place limits on yourself and what you can do? If you would be happier managing a Starbucks, directing plays, grooming dogs, or working as a life coach, why not? If you could move closer to family, make more money, build better balance, or otherwise meet your major life goals through switching careers entirely, again, why not? This is your prerogative—move on, and if you can make your new path work with your financial goals, personality, priorities, and lifestyle, more power to you. It's never too late to turn your interests or passions into a new career.

Moving to a very different field, though, can be more than a little unnerving. One very librarian-like way to ease into a dramatic career change? Do your research! Smooth your entrance into any new field by doing consulting work, subscribing to industry-specific publications, reading articles about the career, joining relevant associations, going on informational interviews, volunteering, and tapping your network of contacts to see if they can put you in touch with someone working in a similar field. Put your library skills to good use by investigating what else you will need to know in your new career. Can you take a course? Read a book? Find part-time or volunteer opportunities to gain on-the-job experience? Join a professional association? Locate a mentor? Go on an informational interview?

Realize also that library skills, whether obviously or not so obviously, transfer to just about every other profession; the ability to organize, retrieve, and interpret information is invaluable in today's knowledge economy. Jobs that at the outset seem quite removed from librarianship may only seem to be strikingly different on the surface, then turn out to utilize many of your library skills as you delve further. So, when making your move, be sure to emphasize the benefits of both your fresh perspective and your transferable skills. As always, many of the skills you have acquired on the job, in school, and through your outside activities transfer to just about any other environment. These will vary widely depending on where you are going, but some broadly useful skills and background include:

- Communication

- Customer service

- Foreign language fluency

- Managing people

- Organizing information

- Research

- Writing

In the following sections, explore a few possibilities and read some stories from librarians who have ranged somewhat further afield. As always, these are just examples—your path is completely open-ended. You can take your career in any direction.

Language Skills

Skills that have been tangential (yet useful) in your library career may be central to your transition into a different type of work. For example, if you are fluent in one or more foreign languages, either as a native speaker or through previous study, perhaps you have used this skill in your library career as a cataloger, or to help with programming or collection development. But your language skills can also transfer to other environments, and you may even wish to consider alternative work as a translator or interpreter.

You can also put your language skills to work to provide value-added services when pursuing many of the other careers discussed throughout this book. You could, for instance, provide foreign-language programming or training, index foreign-language books or articles, or work as an international sales rep for a vendor. Cynthia J. Coan, self-employed indexer, Indexing By the Book, Tucson, AZ, says: "With the rise in recent years in our nation's Spanish-speaking population, publishers are increasingly producing Spanish-language texts, many of which need indexes. Accordingly, I have recently begun marketing my Spanish skills to such publishers in the hope of picking up some business in Spanish-language indexing."

As an info pro, your research background is also useful when doing specialized or written translation. You will need to find out quite a bit about a given subject in order to use the correct contextual terminology. You may be able to use your specific background to specialize in a particular type of translation. Do you have a background as a health sciences librarian? Think about medical translation. A background in business librarianship? Your skills might help you provide effective translations for U.S. companies doing business overseas. Your specific work will depend on the types of documents being translated, ranging from business documents to literature, from legal proceedings to medical documents. You can do freelance translation, work for a translation service, or bring your language skills to a government agency. (Find more on government work in Chapter 3.)

Interpreting is an art unto itself, and you can provide interpreting services to any of a number of institutions, including libraries, hospitals, and government agencies. Whether you work as a sign-language interpreter for library programs or as a Spanish-language interpreter for a local hospital, your background in customer service, your commitment to the privacy of your clients, and your experience working with the public will all be useful.

As with many of the other freelance options open to you, again, working as a translator or interpreter brings an unpredictable workload. You can consider combining this work with another career or providing language-related services as part of an entire package. Resources for interpreters and translators include the American Translators Association (www.atanet.org) and the International Medical Interpreters Association (www.mmia.org/default.asp), as well as local associations across the country. You can also consider pursuing certification through one of these organizations, offering you additional legitimacy and a built-in impetus to keep up your skills.

Writing

Librarians who begin writing for the nonlibrary market have a leg up on other authors thanks to their research abilities and their familiarity with literature and publishing. Whether you write fiction or nonfiction, you'll need to spend quite a bit of time researching your topics and ensuring accuracy in your writing. Your research skills will be useful in a wide range of activities, from interviewing experts to researching a given time period to ensure accurate background and avoid anachronisms to reporting on survey results to poring over records of old court cases.

Your library work and research inevitably inform your writing. Librarian/novelist Ronald M. Gauthier writes in *Library Journal* that "As a library branch manager, I am surrounded by rows of books, periodicals, and compact discs. I traverse mounds of data in electronic format, links pulling me like tentacles into a world illuminated through the wide screens of computers. The library has enriched my storytelling and writing and helped me to take my characters on unforeseen paths, enabling them to become more vivid and real."[2]

You can also look into freelance business or technical writing, where your library skills will definitely be of use and your research skills will allow you to provide value-added services. Janet Bates, self-employed copywriter/secondary researcher, Eagan, MN, explains: "I had been a self-employed Marketing Communications writer for over 10 years when I decided to pursue my MLIS. I had enjoyed working in the school library, I was getting a bit bored with my writing work, and clients were asking for secondary research for their marketing projects just as the Internet was hitting full stride. I really didn't know how to conduct effective research using the Internet and decided to look into an MLIS. I worked on it one class at a time and continued to do my writing work. ... My new research skills helped me add dimension to my writing and offer my customers better value. I also started doing some secondary research projects for my customers." With the economy tanking, Bates was unable to find a traditional library job post-graduation, so she "decided that I could leverage my new skills into my old job, build my business, and make three times the money entry level librarians were being paid—when they could find a job."

Other librarian skills, learned either in school or on the job, may also come in handy, including Web design (to create your own online marketing materials) and computer troubleshooting (you are your own tech support). And if you write books, you can use your knowledge of the library market to help sell your work to libraries, and can use your experience with programming to market yourself as a visiting author or writing workshop leader.

Beyond writing fiction or nonfiction books, you can also employ your writing, research, and analysis skills as a freelance writer in magazine and/or online markets. Many sites list freelance opportunities for writers, but some major resources include:

- craigslist, www.craigslist.org (check listings in both your geographical area and the larger metropolitan areas like San Francisco, which tend to include location-independent ads)

- FreelanceWriting.com, www.freelancewriting.com/freelance-writing-jobs.php

- mediabistro.com's Freelance Marketplace, www.mediabistro.com/fm

For the Love of the Story

I fell into being an author. I never thought of pursuing it professionally; I just wrote a book for fun. Once I was finished, I liked it enough to send it to the publishing house that had published my favorite YA books when I was young, and one of the editors there contacted me. Now, I write original manuscripts and then revise them under the direction of the editor at my publishing house who has chosen to work with me. Editors and authors try to form long-term relationships, so although I've written and sold six and a half manuscripts, I've only worked with two editors. Revision is a collaborative pursuit; neither the author nor the editor takes complete charge of the course of a book. I have deadlines to meet, and I have to give every revision my full attention no matter how inopportune the timing might be. (The copyeditor's remarks for my next novel, for instance, came back for work right in the middle of my transatlantic move!)

In addition to the writing work, I respond to business concerns that my agent brings up, such as reading and signing contracts. I also take time to respond to the readers who contact me, and answer queries from teachers, book club members, reviewers, and librarians. I maintain my Web site, which is something many authors do because we love the chance to talk directly to our readers, without the filter of agents or editors. I contribute to a forum on writing that is available to amateur writers, and answer letters from people seeking advice on starting a writing career.

Writing books, reading books, and treasuring books are all facets of the same passion. Librarians are guardians of our culture, and libraries are meeting grounds between past and future thinkers. In an curious way, so are novels: We writers pick the most important ideas from the books we have treasured and meditate upon those ideas as we create our own works, passing them along to the next generation of readers.

Of course, the classes I took in children's librarianship and YA lit paid off handsomely. So did the mindset that librarianship builds in its professionals: the willingness to collaborate. Writers and editors have to get along and deal with tough issues as we revise, and we have to do almost all of that work as part of a long-distance relationship. I don't think I'd be successful if I saw my relationship with my editors as a power struggle. I had to get used to working closely over email or phone with people who are thousands of miles away, people I only see once every few years, or even never.

Becoming a successful novelist can be easy, or it can be impossible. The competition is comparable to that in professional sports, but then, so is the payoff. For those who want to join me on the bookstore and library shelves, I'd say be honest with yourself and compare your manuscript to what's on the bestseller lists right now. Don't review it like an author, review it like a librarian: Your work has to be top notch. On the other hand, don't tailor what you write to what you think the market wants. Write for yourself, for the love of the story. Write the book you can't wait to read, and your delight will be infectious. The best part is the chance to laugh at my own jokes! I write first and foremost for my own amusement, and I've been very lucky that my work has amused other people, too. Lines that I wrote years ago still make me chuckle today.

Worst is the gradual shift of something I loved into something I have to do. I'm lucky enough to do what I love for a living, but that inevitably affects how I feel about it. As Moliere once said, "Writing is like prostitution. First you do it for love, and then for a few close friends, and then for money." Now that I do it for money, and now that I know that my work will be picked apart by hostile reviewers, I have a hard time losing myself in it anymore.

I also miss the companionship. Authors write in isolation, whereas in the library, I was never alone. I miss the group identity, the feeling that we are building a great institution for our clientele. When an author stands up to speak, she's alone, and I find that very hard. I do stay in touch with what my friends are publishing, and love the chance to read the reviews and go visit libraries and library conferences. I don't, however, miss unlocking my office at 8 AM. It's nice to be able to do my work at home!

Clare B. Dunkle is a YA book author, published currently with Henry Holt & Co. and Atheneum Press (Simon & Schuster).

Other resources for writers include the National Writers Union (NWU; www.nwu.org), the American Society of Journalists and Authors (ASJA; www.asja.org), and Inkygirl: Daily Diversions for Writers (www.inkygirl.com). Be sure also to go to your local library and peruse the most recent edition of *The Writer's Market* for additional markets and advice.

When writing for publication outside the library field, you draw on many of the same skills and techniques as when writing for the profession (see Chapter 4). Editors in any field appreciate authors who can follow guidelines, write to deadline, and show that they have an understanding of the type of material a given publisher is looking for. Put your research skills to work by researching the publication you are targeting. Read back issues; familiarize yourself with its guidelines, its target audience, its tone and style. Don't let the truism "write what you know" limit you to the library literature.

Think instead about writing what you can find out—you're a librarian; you can research anything!

Outside Activities

When information professionals build on what they love to do, they may find themselves moving from their job in a library toward building a new career out of a hobby, a passion, or volunteer work. As librarians, we love to categorize things. We often place "volunteer work" and "hobbies" into a separate box, when in fact these activities can easily spill over to the world of "work" or "career." Embrace fluidity and allow yourself to envision building a life from these outside activities.

Where in Chapter 1 you thought about your work-related strengths, here think about what you are good at, what you are interested in, and what you love to do, without regard for whether these are related to your current career. Don't censor yourself: Focus on your interests and hobbies, and open your mind to the notion that these can expand into other areas of your life. Take your own interests seriously. You may be a gifted amateur photographer, a musician, a crafter or knitter, or gardener. You may enjoy teaching Sunday school, or your friends may all turn to you for advice on interior decorating. Think of the areas in which others consider you an expert. Are you the go-to person for advice on child raising? On cooking? On home repair?

Beyond hobbies, look at your volunteer work, at church, at a nonprofit, at an environmental organization. This work stems out of a commitment to a cause or an organization; many people go on to build careers out of their commitment, and their passion for a cause becomes the basis for their new path. You need, however, to be genuinely committed to your volunteer work—don't just offer your services to a given organization as a networking ploy, as your intentions will be transparent.

Adventures in Association Management

My path to my new career was unplanned. In order to get my teaching credential to work in the Illinois public schools, I needed a bunch of fill-in general requirements; one was PE. I got into a class called "Introduction to Adventure Education" with no idea what I was in for, and the path turned completely to one side. I became involved in Experiential Education (EE) organizations as a volunteer, and used whatever I could in my school situation. Eventually, I could no longer hack the public schools, and worked on developing other options involving working more in EE. I worked for a Massachusetts-based nonprofit for three years, was downsized—then this job came open, and I have been here for the last 5 years.

This work speaks to me because of the way I was educated, and because I have seen firsthand the difference it can make in someone's life. Most of us do this work because of our own experience in going through some kind of adventure program (in terms of adventure education, not a classic "adventure"), and because we see the possibilities for helping others. The educational methodology cuts across all learning styles, and is a good fit for those with learning disabilities as well.

I'm basically an administrator—I engage in a lot of public interaction, which is a reference interview most of the time! I write a lot, help write and edit our newsletter, manage projects and people (especially volunteers), plan meetings, and manage a budget. I am very attached to the mission of our organization, and would not be interested in a general career in association management (which is what my current job is called). I miss exposure to new books, but I use the public library extensively. I miss being with students, but I don't miss the public school environment.

I do miss the face-to-face people connections, in a great setting, but love working from a home office. My interactions now are mostly via email and phone. There are some days I wish I had a cart of books to shelve, or a group of catalogs to clean out—there is very little of that kind of work in my current job!

My library work did help prepare me for this job. For one thing, I know exactly what it's like to go home every night without the feeling that I got to the end of my list, or that tomorrow there will be carts of books to shelve again. I also learned how to manage projects, through doing just that—no one ever taught me.

Sylvia Dresser is Executive Director, Association for Challenge Course Technology, Deerfield, IL.

You might decide to build an alternative career out of an outside interest or hobby precisely because it differs so much from librarianship. One survey respondent who now works as a vendor and performer at Renaissance festivals explains: "Initially, it looked like, and was, a lot of fun, notably because of the total contrast between my regular job and faire work. Also, after nearly 20 years as a faculty member, I was beginning to look for new learning experiences. I am still learning a lot. And, aside from such things as fire ants in Florida, tornados in the Midwest, thunderstorms in a lot of places, and the other aspects of living in the outdoors and traveling a lot, it's still fun much of the time."

You can start out by turning your hobby, interest, volunteer work, or passion into a side job or secondary career, which allows you to experiment and progress without the pressure of making money right away. Consider this option when thinking about various types of blended careers discussed in Chapter 4.

Other Options

Some alternative careers seem more directly related to library work than others. Careers that draw in some way on your library and research skills—and that might seem more or less directly related to librarianship, depending on your perspective—include:

- *Association management* – While work in library associations is discussed in Chapter 2, you can also range further afield and bring your project management, nonprofit, and management skills to bear in nonlibrary associations as well—or bring your passion for the work of that association in to play. (See the sidebar on page 167.)

- *Paralegal* – Research, organization, abstracting, cataloging—all of these familiar skills inform your work as a paralegal. You may choose to move from law librarianship or research into this field. Think about earning a certificate in the field or otherwise continuing your education to make yourself more marketable. (See the sidebar on page 170.)

- *Private investigator* – Like an information broker, a private investigator can specialize in particular areas (adoption, missing persons). You will need to get a license from your state and to meet all other governmental requirements (usually including a background check, fingerprints, a bond, and a business license). Some states require PIs to have a law enforcement background. Here, skills in research, genealogy, and data collection—as well as patience—can all be useful.

Don't limit yourself to these few suggestions. Think about other options that on the surface seem completely unrelated to the work you do as a librarian, but that also require research, data analysis, and information organization skills.

Progressing as a Paralegal

I worked in libraries (school and university) from the time I was 10 until I completed my library school coursework at age 23. After I finished my MLS, I was overqualified for the para-professional positions I had held prior to receiving my degree—yet I had no professional experience, so no one would hire me for professional positions either. After spending more than a year working for minimum wage and another year working for $7.00/hour (while applying for library jobs, interviewing all over the eastern half of the country, and exhausting all the job options in the small county where we lived), my husband and I moved 700 miles away for a fresh start.

A week after our move, I answered an ad in the local newspaper for a project assistant position that sounded like it would make good use of my cataloging, indexing, and abstracting skills. I wound up temping at a law firm, then progressed to a permanent position as a paralegal. After a few years, I went back to school for a post-baccalaureate certificate program in legal studies. I am now a litigation paralegal. So, I fell into this field, but it's done well by me—and I use my cataloging, indexing, abstracting, and reference skills on a daily basis. I also use much of what I learned about information technology in my daily life at a small firm, where I am also the IT department!

I am responsible for procuring, organizing, indexing, and abstracting medical records and others proofs of damages for personal injury clients. I also do legal research, both in books and online databases, and draft legal documents, including memoranda of law and briefs. I like being able to use my library skills in my daily work and I like being treated like a professional member of the legal services team. I prefer the atmosphere of an academic library, however, and the regular hours that come with such a job. I miss the freedom of an academic setting; people are more tolerant there. I have progressed far enough in the paralegal field over the last 10 years that I now make a much higher salary than I would as a librarian, however, and that would be hard to give up at this point.

If you would like to be a law librarian, you need the JD as well as the MLS. If, however, you want to use your library skills without incurring the expense of another post-graduate degree, a paralegal certificate program (which usually requires 8–10 courses) can be very helpful in preparing you for a rewarding career as a paralegal.

Jay-Jay Flanagan-Grannemann is Office Manager/Legal Assistant, Law Offices of W. Ralph Garris, P.A., Columbia, SC.

Sometimes we fall into our alternative careers, and then realize that they are actually a better match for our skills and personalities than librarianship ever was. Other times these nontraditional career paths let us avoid the drawbacks inherent in our particular field of librarianship, whether this be local politics, bureaucracy, or low pay. Our skills as info pros underpin our careers, no matter what path we choose.

Think about what you would have been had you not chosen or fallen into libraries. What have you always wished you could do? What did you do before you entered the profession? Which friends, colleagues, or acquaintances do you secretly envy? When you close your eyes, where do you envision yourself? Where would you work if you had the "right" education, experience, background? An openness to potential and a passion for your new path, wherever it may lead, go a long way toward making your ideal career possible.

Endnotes

1. David Weinberger, *Everything Is Miscellaneous: The Power of the New Digital Disorder*, New York: Henry Holt, 2007: 230.

2. Ronald M. Gauthier, "Librarian, Or Author?" *Library Journal* August 15, 2007, www.libraryjournal.com/article/CA6466635.html (accessed October 12, 2007).

Chapter 8

Working in IT Outside of Libraries

... there is a world of opportunities out there for information professionals. But, if we want the opportunities, we might have to look outside the predefined IP world sometimes, and not be too precious about people knowing what an IP is. Staying in the confines of the IP world is safe, and for some will deliver a long and happy career. But if you fancy a change or a challenge you may need to take what seems like a step away.[1]

As some LIS programs have become more IT-intensive, and as info pros have acquired (out of either necessity or interest) the technology skills to succeed in their current careers, many find that they can also transfer these skills to the more lucrative corporate world. The line between information work and IT work can be very thin, and blended roles in search, KM, information architecture, and other often technology-heavy information fields are discussed in Chapter 6. It is also possible, though, to move from library work to more traditional IT positions, where your background as an info pro is an asset, but less obviously central to your new career. The overlap between information work and IT doesn't stop at the door of the library; information workers and managers of information in various industries carry out both librarian-like and technology-related duties. Further, librarians' skills in areas like technology instruction and troubleshooting transfer directly to other environments, as does a background or coursework in related fields like HCI (human computer interaction), information architecture, and usability.

When making the decision about where best to deploy your IT skills, your priorities come into play:

- If the library environment is important to you—its non-profit, people-centered, or community service aspects—but you for one reason or another need to move on, you may wish to investigate IT work with nonprofits, governmental entities, or other institutions that are similar in some way to libraries. (Find more in Chapter 3 on working in similar organizations.)

- If you find you like IT work for its own sake, the type of institution you work in may be less important; just seek a position that matches your skills and interests.

- If you wish to earn market rates for your IT skills, and you have the requisite certification and background, you will wish to investigate larger corporations and avoid the library field and nonprofits.

- If you appreciate the overlap between librarianship and IT, you might look for positions that tap into those intersections and call on your skills with both technology and information.

- If you appreciate the flexibility or the regular hours offered by library IT work, as opposed to IT work in a corporate environment, you may actually wish to rethink your initial decision to leave!

IT positions include job titles ranging from network administrator to technology trainer to software engineer to Webmaster—and the leap from, say, a library Webmaster or network administrator to a for-profit Webmaster or network administrator is not as far as one might imagine. Librarians moving into the corporate world often find they can combine their IT and info pro skills in fields such as managing information systems (MIS), or find that their facility with both technology and information lends itself well to blended roles such as information architect (see Chapter 6) or user interface designer. Some LIS schools are starting to take advantage of these trends, especially those that have transformed themselves into "schools of information" and dropped the library nomenclature altogether. These schools offer blended degrees, certificates in related areas, and technology-intensive coursework, and can be a good choice for those interested in both technology and information work. (See more on changes in LIS education in Chapter 11, Where To from Here?)

Transferable skills, experiences, and qualities for those moving into IT work include:

- Communication
- Management
- Organization
- Problem solving
- Project management
- Research
- Specific technical skills and experience (network administration, Web design, troubleshooting, programming, etc.)
- Team-building
- Training
- User-centered focus
- Vendor contract negotiation

You can also use the customer-focused skills you have built up through your work in libraries to help you serve as the bridge between IT and the rest of an organization—so-called soft skills can be more important to success in some IT positions than technical skills, which can always be learned. Your reference interview skills transfer in allowing you to get to the heart of what your users truly want to accomplish with technology. Your public service skills transfer in helping you keep a user-centered focus, keeping technology centered on the goals of your organization and the success of its people, rather than seeing it as an end in itself.

Those interested in managing technology or techie staff, rather than in hands-on programming, development, or other IT positions, still need to develop a broad understanding of the field and the ability to understand relevant terminology. As one survey respondent notes: "You don't have to be an IT person per se to work in a tech-heavy role, but you need to understand the ins and outs of database design and management to suggest new data flows in your products and services. Also, don't stop learning. You should learn new things every day that enhance your value."

Creating Equitable Access

When I graduated library school, my previous work experience all centered on writing server and client-side Web programs. I was interested in being a librarian and providing online services similar to those I encountered as an undergraduate, but my experience searching for this kind of work led me to believe that senior librarians with a lot of experience working as "regular" librarians generally staffed technology positions.

It appeared I'd have to spend a lot of time as a traditional Librarian I, then work my way up the ladder. Because I had no prior traditional library experience, and because the competition was intense (public libraries in my area had MLS graduates working as pages and waiting up to two years for a Librarian I opening), I didn't go that route. Through people I knew, I was able to find work doing what I wanted (sort of—

the development side at least) much more quickly than if I had jumped into the library profession.

At Ask.com, I am a user interface engineer. I work on Bloglines as part of a team, creating the widgets and interface elements that users use to interact with the application. I develop using JavaScript and CSS, relying heavily on Dojo, a very powerful JavaScript library, and also work to ensure accessibility and cross-browser compatibility. We all work together to come to a consensus on the user interface and overall application design, but most of my time is spent as a developer.

I like developing, creating user interfaces, and problem solving. We work with a lot of information we have to present in a user friendly way. Many of the tools out there, especially in electronic library tools and searchable databases, have terrible user interfaces that don't take advantage of modern JavaScript and the opportunities available to network and connect people in innovative ways. So, I appreciate working in an industry on the cutting edge, where new ideas and new ways of doing things are encouraged, where we expand the possibilities of what you can do with browsers and in the context of a networked world.

My alternative career pays significantly better than similar work in librarianship, and that's a plus. What I like least is that I'm not really working in the setting I envisioned. I was a little disappointed at the closed nature of information (DRM, license agreements) in the academic/library environment; this feels like the antithesis of what libraries were built for. As librarians, we should be connecting all this information, making it easier to find and consume information, break new boundaries, and provide access. I work for a search engine, so maybe I'll have a chance to do this someday—even if not as a librarian.

My MLS program included a class on User Interfaces and Human Computer Interfaces, something I'm doing now. Quality metadata, thinking about accessibility, cultural issues, organizing information, user interfaces, ethics, decision making, and management are all relevant. Very few of my courses at SIRLS (University of Arizona) even discussed what I imagined would be traditional librarian roles. I didn't take classes on selecting books for children, creating a special collection, or cataloging. Even much of my reference services class applies to what I do now—at Bloglines, we satisfy users' information needs. That's our mission. A lot of the problems we face involve managing and providing access to a high volume of information, which is also analogous to librarianship in many ways. Bloglines is a free service, so I feel as if I'm still working as an information professional to create equitable access.

A lot of the skills required for what I do now, though, are not taught in an MLS program. Computer science, algorithms, programming languages, networking, and other technology-intensive skills were only discussed in distant and abstract terms at SIRLS. A few of the courses required assignments to be turned in as HTML, but that really just scratches the surface of the skills required. My coworkers all have a computer science background, and I think my MLS background is an asset to the team. But, without my previous experience in development, I would not be able to work in my current position.

I do miss working in a library. For all my love and belief in a digital information future, I miss working in a place filled with books and students and librarians.

Bjorn Tipling is a Software Engineer, Bloglines at Ask.com, San Jose, CA.

Many librarians move into or remain in corporate IT mainly because of the potential for higher salaries outside of libraries. One survey respondent suggests: "I would say, if you enjoy it, focus on technology. I make more money now than I would with an MLS in an academic library setting. A lot more. I'm just thankful that I didn't get the degree before discovering my current position." Many, though, do remain conflicted about this choice. If you think you may someday wish to take the salary cut and move back to libraries, be sure to keep up your contacts and your professional memberships. You may want to volunteer part-time in a local library, read library blogs and journals, and/or stay active in professional associations in order to remain connected to the profession. Your IT skills will come in handy in keeping connected, as well—libraries can always use volunteer technology trainers; association subgroups can always use Webmasters.

Building Skills

Alternatively, if you wish to move into IT outside libraries but currently work in a less obviously technology-oriented position, think about ways to bolster your skills and show that you have the relevant background and expertise to take on an IT role. (See more on technology-related jobs inside libraries, as well as ideas on increasing your IT skills, in Chapter 9, Nontraditional Roles, Traditional Institutions.) Beef up your techie credentials by joining library-related technology organizations like ASIS&T (www.asis. org) and LITA (www.lita.org); use their resources, publications, conferences, and workshops to expand your skills before moving on.

Many IT positions, though, do require more intensive skills and background than you can generally pick up from library-related workshops and seminars. You can consider going back to school to earn a degree or certificate in the field you're targeting, taking CE courses at a local community college, or pursuing certification.

User Friendly

I started library school as a Web designer, trying to learn more about information architecture as a way to augment my career. So, I guess you could say I went to library school already planning to enter an alternative career. (I also would love to work in a public library one day!)

Soon after I started at Simmons, I had the opportunity to transition into work as a user interface designer. I continued in library school because I thought there was a lot to learn about metadata, systems analysis, and related topics, and I was able to take a fair number of courses around Web development and specification in library school. I also had the opportunity to get involved with groups like the local ASIST chapter, which broadened my awareness of the field. Knowledge of graphic design and how Web applications are built, though, were key to my later development in this career, and those things I learned outside of library school.

I love user interface design, because you can see how your work helps people understand how to use software. I've watched my designs go through usability testing, and it's rewarding to watch successive testers have an easier time accomplishing their goals. I guess it's that satisfaction that has kept me at it. Just as in librarianship, there is an emphasis on access to information and organizing information in a way that makes it easy for people to find and use. In a typical day I might:

- Create wireframes showing how Web applications should look
- Attend design review meetings to contribute to the work of other designers

- Conduct usability tests on one of the applications we're working on
- Attend development meetings to keep up with projects' progress and help solve problems
- Write specifications for developers describing how an application should work

In this field, experience is the most important thing—more important than any degree. In order to get experience, it's worth finding ways to get involved with the Web presence of professional organizations, charities, schools—anywhere you can. Back up the work you do on these sites with usability testing. Document your work on a personal portfolio Web site. Library school is a great place to do this, and many schools will get you started with the skills you need to do basic Web development and usability testing.

I would love to work in a library one day; the main thing that has held me back is money. I get paid well in the software business, and would lose a big chunk of my salary if I worked in a library. I am the sole earner in my family right now, so that is not an option. I am inspired by public libraries and would love to one day be able to help libraries work on improving access to their Internet services.

Ben Brophy is Senior User Interface Designer, ATG, Inc., Cambridge, MA.

Another alternative is simply using books, online tutorials, or hands-on practice to start learning on your own. If your targeted field requires programming experience, you'll need to identify the languages most often used in that field and bone up on them. If the field requires network administration, set up a small LAN in your home, shadow your library's network administrator, and/or take an online course. If it requires Web design skills, volunteer to work on your library's site or to create a site for a local organization, create an online portfolio for yourself, investigate online tutorials, and familiarize yourself with current standards. Envision your ideal technology-related work, then take steps to gain the skills you need to get there.

If you already have a number of IT responsibilities in your library, look into technology certifications you can pursue that will demonstrate your knowledge and experience; check your own academic or public library for study guides. If you have, for instance, spent years as a Windows network administrator, think about testing for your MCSE (www.microsoft.com/learning/mcp/mcse/default.mspx) or MCSA (www.microsoft.com/learning/mcp/mcsa/default.mspx). If your duties include troubleshooting and PC repair, go ahead and test for your CompTIA A+ certification (certification.comptia.org/a/default.aspx). Nonlibrary organizations recognize and value these and other technical certifications, allowing you to gain credit for your accomplishments and transfer your skills more easily.

Also make sure that your library job title accurately reflects your current duties, which can be an issue when you go to move on. In libraries, we often take on additional tasks beyond the original scope of our job titles and descriptions. If you design your library's Web site, maintain its network, or provide technology training to its patrons, but your official job title is reference librarian or head of circulation, talk to your administration about expanding your title to encompass your new duties. Even if this involves a cumbersome title like reference librarian/Webmaster or children's librarian/technology trainer, push for an official recognition of your role that better reflects your actual work; you may be grateful in the future. Emphasize specific technology-related skills, experience, and accomplishments on your resume, and consider creating a functional resume to better highlight your skills. (More on functional resumes in Appendix A.)

Keeping It in the Family

You can also parlay the skills and recognition you gain in your library into a technology-related position in your larger institution, organization, or local government. Officials or committees familiar with your work may be very open to your application, or may even actively recruit you for such a role. Most employers prefer internal candidates: You're a known quantity; they don't have to go to the expense and bother of an outside search; and you'll take less training and hand-holding before you get up to speed in your new position and duties.

Out of Anonymity

I more or less taught myself HTML in 1992, *before* there was a graphical Web browser. I still remember my amazement in learning the image tag and seeing the image show up in Mosaic. Over time, I became increasingly responsible for library technology. I created our library's first Web site; I created a Web-based architectural history image database; I ran our library's ILS; I taught myself ColdFusion and did a lot of hard-core coding of some interesting applications (that I presented at various conferences); I won a NJ-ACLR Technology Innovation Award. When the library was asked to "consult" on the university's Web site relaunch strategy, my boss asked me to fill that role. Three months later, when our president asked to form a new office of University Web Services, I was asked to lead that office.

Now, I am responsible for our university's public Web site. Its main focus is on recruitment and enrollment, and my office reports directly to our university's president. I partner with our University Communications people on one hand and our university IT people on the other hand. I try to direct our "big picture" Web strategy, while also managing our relaunch project (which is equal parts technical, design, content, and political). I'm able to have techie conversations with my tech team in the morning, then Web marketing strategy conversations with higher university officials in the afternoon.

I most like the challenges we are meeting and the problems we are solving. The work is challenging, but we are coming up with solutions. I also appreciate seeing the team (my department) that I've cultivated and given a new "culture" (of innovation, pride, enthusiasm, collaboration) work together, develop ideas and programs, and achieve success. What I like least is the bureaucracy and the administrative paperwork!

Some people are puzzled when they hear [that I went from] "librarian to Web director." To me, it makes perfect sense. When NJIT senior staff created their proposal to form an office of University Web Services, they wrote that the director of that office would need these skills:

- Management experience
- Innovative use of technology
- Web-based service orientation
- Information architecture and user-interface design
- Effective communicator

These are exactly the skills I cultivated as Assistant University Librarian in charge of our digital innovation and technology.

My career continues to be related to librarianship in terms of:

- Organization of knowledge
- Information architecture
- Technology management
- Paying attention to users
- Customer-service focus
- User-interface design

In 2001, I led our library's ILS migration; I find parallels in our migration from one Web site Content Management System (CMS) to another. I had been coding library applications based on API/Web services/SOA approaches; we are still taking some of these approaches on the entire university Web site.

I did have to learn our Web site CMS and expand my knowledge of budgeting. I also had to emerge from the relative anonymity of the library to the bright glare of the entire university looking at me for results in our Web site relaunch. So I had to learn to be more attuned to the politics and strategic plans and directions of the entire university—and I'm still learning. I wish I had had more time and less pressure to make the transition. As it was, the new department was formed in the eleventh hour with a specific mandate to "get the site relaunched ASAP." Of course, that's a Catch 22. There would never have been a new department formed [out of] whole cloth if there weren't a "crisis" of sorts.

Maybe, in retrospect, I was ready to move on and apply some of my ideas to a larger venue. I don't miss book-buying budget oversight. I don't miss circulation desk scheduling. I don't miss meetings about journal cancellations. I don't miss overseeing cataloging operations. I was happiest developing Web applications for our library, and that's (sort of) what I'm continuing to do now, on a larger scale.

> I do miss the people and the library culture, and some-times joke that "I'll always be a librarian," and, "you can take the boy out of the library, but you can't take the library out of the boy."
>
> *Jim Robertson is Director of University Web Services, NJIT (New Jersey Institute of Technology), Newark, NJ.*

Leveraging your tech skills to move on, either into local government or within your own institution, allows you to base yourself in the familiar while also tackling new challenges and stretching your career in new directions. This also allows you to continue working in a similar environment, which may better match your career goals and personal values than would moving to a new institution or into a corporate environment.

Most libraries are part of a larger institution or governmental entity, giving you built-in opportunities for advancement. Take some time to lay the groundwork by building networks with people outside your library and its niche. Volunteer for technology-related committees. See how library technology relates to and integrates with the larger organization. You face the same challenges here as anyone else moving into municipal management or into another job in their local government or institution: to prove yourself, prove your skills, and prove that library experience is applicable in the larger world.

Endnotes

1. Helen Day, "I'm an Information Professional—But What Next?: Where Can Your IP Skills Take You?" *Business Information Review* 23:3 (2006): 195.

Chapter 9

Nontraditional Roles, Traditional Institutions

Nontraditional professional positions are not only growing in size and influence; they also pay more. Compensation for traditional library professionals has long lagged as a result of their relatively weak market value outside libraries. But that is not the case for IT specialists, fund raisers, financial and human-resource professionals, and so on.[1]

Nontraditional positions within libraries encompass a number of jobs with titles such as repository librarian, metadata librarian, digital librarian, Webmaster, emerging technologies librarian, electronic resources librarian, and digitization librarian. In many cases, these types of jobs are either enabled or necessitated by technological advances; most were unimaginable, or at least uncommon, even a short 10 years back. As our perceptions of librarianship and what exactly the field encompasses change slowly, librarians working in these roles are still seen as nontraditional by many colleagues and administrators.

Students now entering library school have the benefit of seeing these newer roles as career options from the beginning. If you enter the field open to the possibility of working in these types of positions, you expand your horizons and your potential—including your earning potential. Current librarians who want to stay in libraries, but are burned out on the same old reference, cataloging, or children's duties, can take steps to acquire the skills necessary to step into these positions. The day-to-day work of those in nontraditional library positions may differ greatly from the day-to-day work in more traditional jobs, yet each draws on the practices and principles of librarianship.

The following sections also discuss careers in areas like library grant writing and human resources, as well as other nontraditional positions within traditional institutions that depend less on technological change than on people's diverse experiences, abilities, education, and backgrounds. These types of jobs can be a great way to remain in the library environment while still branching out to use a different set of skills or drawing on your previous nonlibrary education or background.

Tangled in Technology

Much of the growth in nontraditional career opportunities for librarians has been occurring inside traditional libraries, largely due to the need for staff who have the ability to work effectively with newer technology. We now see ads with verbiage like:

- *Web Services Librarian*: Wanted! A digital native to take the Library to Web 2.0 and beyond. Do you blog, IM, or wiki? Must be able to envision how these and other emerging technologies can be used to create excellent patron service.

- *Emergent Technologies Librarian*: The Emergent Technologies Librarian will serve as an explorer of and advocate for the use of emergent technologies to support online learning and enhance the effectiveness of library information and instructional services.

- *Web Content Manager and Designer*: Responsible for managing library Web site and intranet and may also design and construct Web pages. Maintains ongoing design of the Web site. Writes, develops, designs, edits, and proofreads new content/services. Requirements: MLS from ALA-accredited institution.

- *Virtual Branch Manager:* Position Qualifications: Master's Degree in Library Science from an academically accredited college or university and three (3) years of public library experience which includes 2 years of supervisory experience and experience using current technologies such as Dreamweaver, Flash, Fireworks, various Adobe products, ASP.Net, Visual Basic.Net, Ajax, ColdFusion, Perl, JavaScripting, and Cascading Style Sheets.

- *Emerging & New Technology Librarian:* Looking for an energetic library professional who can apply updated practices and perspectives to a traditional reference setting. Seeking a person who will evaluate, teach, coordinate, and implement new and emerging technologies, will coordinate the overhaul of our existing Web site, and who understands 2.0 as a service concept, not just a tech thing.

- *Immersive Learning Librarian (aka "Gaming Librarian"):* Seeking a creative, innovative and experienced librarian to provide leadership in establishing [our] Library as the premier North American academic library in the implementation of innovative, highly engaging, habitable environments for teaching and learning. This includes the development and support of educationally sound virtual worlds, simulations and games. ... The successful candidate will be responsible for conceiving, designing, implementing, operating, and evaluating innovative teaching and learning environments relevant to the campus community.

- *Technology Integration Librarian:* The individual's main responsibility is to provide technical expertise in delivering information to a global internal client base. Candidate will develop and maintain databases and applications, integrate current and future systems and maintain and troubleshoot technical aspects of critical library information tools.

(All examples excerpted from jobs posted online during Winter–Summer, 2007.)

Any technological experience and skills will come in handy in a library job search, since nearly every librarian now uses technology on a day-to-day basis. However, specialized or in-demand skills lead to increased—and more nontraditional—opportunities. Paying attention to the changing job market, even if you are presently solidly employed, helps you keep your skills current and see where the field may be headed. Market yourself for technology-related positions in libraries by showing how your library background, education, and outlook make you a more valuable candidate than IT people who lack this perspective. Take time on a regular basis to browse the ads on LISjobs.com or your local library job database; note how position titles and duties change over time.

Open Access and Digital Repositories

After dropping out of a PhD program in 1998, by pure serendipity I landed at a small publishing-services bureau—editing, typesetting, and digital conversion for STM publishers and university presses. I loved the work, and was absolutely entranced by the potential of electronic text, from books for the print-disabled to text mining in linguistic research.

In 2002, very much wanting to continue working with electronic text but thoroughly burned out on publishers in general and the ebook industry in particular, I asked myself who else was doing the kind of work I loved. The answer, of course, was "academic libraries," and so I overcame my jitters at the thought of returning to graduate school and applied to UW-Madison. My first semester there, I took a course in "virtual collection development" that introduced me to the serials crisis and the emerging open-access movement. I was hooked again—I am easily hooked by noble crusades—though I did not then realize I could make a career for myself in that area, and was planning to go into digitization or library Web development instead.

I did come into library school with many useful computer-related skills, including basic programming and Web design. That's just as well, because library school offered few opportunities to learn them. I say this as a caution to those considering digital-library careers: Do not expect library school to teach you much about the nitty-gritty of working with computers! Get those skills on your own if you do not already have them.

As for the rest of library school, the database class I took sure comes in handy! Mass-editing metadata in DSpace is a tedious chore, but SQL makes it almost a pleasure. What I learned about metadata standards and their raisons d'etre has also been of considerable use to me, as was the introduction to information architecture that has informed my DSpace redesign efforts. I also needed the socialization into the profession that library school offered me. I would have been at sea without it; I have to understand my colleagues, their work, and their attitudes, in order to work well with them and get my job done.

I was extremely fortunate after graduation to land a job at George Mason University running their new institutional repository. I started at Mason without a shred of Java programming or systems-administration experience. That changed in a hurry. I also had to develop my people-handling and marketing skills; I'm better than I used to be, but there's still room for improvement.

A year and a half later, I happily came home to Madison to run the MINDS@UW repository, which serves all 26 campuses of the state university system. At UWDCC, I am half outreach coordinator, half digital preservationist, half project manager, half copyright manager, and one-quarter programmer and Web designer—and yes, that does add up to more than the whole!

As outreach coordinator, I promote MINDS@UW to faculty and other librarians to encourage deposit of content. I train people on the MINDS@UW user interface. I also sit on committees and act as liaison to various technologists and technology groups, who control an awful lot of content that I would like to see deposited.

As project manager, I help set MINDS@UW policies and procedures, keep various people and committees apprised of what is happening with MINDS@UW, and carry out tasks and projects assigned to me. I also perform batch imports of large quantities of material to save time for others.

As digital preservationist, I advise on file formats and perform conversions or other touchups (such as bringing other people's HTML into line with published standards) to material destined for MINDS@UW. Keeping up-to-date is a major responsibility here, as file formats and methods for coping with them change quickly.

As copyright manager, I advise faculty how much of their work may legally be deposited into MINDS@UW, and in what form. Should there ever be a copyright challenge to MINDS@UW material, I will be responsible for resolving it without getting the UW System into legal trouble.

As programmer and Web designer, I tweak the DSpace software that powers MINDS@UW to my liking, although I haven't done much of that yet in my current position because I have to wait for a major user-interface platform change. I also diagnose, report, and (when I can) fix software bugs, and lend a hand on the DSpace support mailing lists.

Within the profession, I have occasionally had to cope with an odd sort of envy. Scholarly communication and digital librarianship are growth fields within academic librarianship, and a few academic librarians appear to believe that I jumped on an opportunity they regret missing, although I hasten to say that I chose this field because of personal affinities and interests rather than any sense that it was the new cool thing. (Indeed, it's far from clear that institutional repositories are a sustainable innovation. I may yet find myself out of a job!) At its worst, this envy becomes outright hostility.

Librarianship is still deciding how it wants to react to computers. Some librarians (prominently, Michael Gorman and Rory Litwin) genuinely believe that computer programming is not something librarians should do. As one who vigorously champions the opposite view—computers are useful tools in librarianship, just as reference interviews and AACR2 are useful tools, and librarians should collectively master the profession's useful tools—I sometimes find it very hard to establish common ground with colleagues who dislike computers or fear their impact on the profession.

I derive immense personal satisfaction from my work. The open-access movement holds real promise for improving the entire world through rapid and unfettered dissemination of human knowledge, and though I am only a small part of the movement, what I do is significant. That said, the open-access movement in general and self-archiving in particular are progressing very slowly, which is nothing if not frustrating. Faculty ignorance and apathy, librarian ignorance and apathy, fear-uncertainty-and-doubt, vigorous publisher opposition—I have to live with a lot of setbacks and outright failures, and keep coming back strong.

Most of what I do can be learned on the job (and, in fact, that's where I learned a lot of it). The hard part is demonstrating aptitude for a potential employer. Get some real computer skills, learn your metadata standards, and if you're genuinely interested in this field, keep up on events in scholarly communication and copyright and be ready to discuss them. The *SPARC Open Access Newsletter* is the easiest way to do so; also keep an eye on *D-Lib* and *Ariadne* for repository-related articles.

Dorothea Salo is Digital Repository Librarian, University of Wisconsin Digital Collections Center (UWDCC), Madison, WI.

Technology enables the expansion of library work into realms from Web design to emerging technologies. If one of these technology-related careers looks interesting, find ways to gain the experience and skills necessary to pursue it. If you are interested in becoming a Web developer, for example, volunteer to work on your own library's site, or to create or redesign one for a smaller local library, nonprofit organization, club, or local organization. Read Julie Still's *The Accidental Webmaster* (ITI, 2003). Check out books on Web design and development, practice with current technologies, work with online tutorials, download trial versions of software and throw yourself into exploring its features. Create a personal Web site highlighting your skills and projects. Take courses at your local library school or community college. Take workshops offered by local library systems or at your institution. (Find more on continuing education in

Making Myself Marketable

While completing my MLS degree, I took as many Web and electronic-related courses as possible. However, it was difficult to find jobs in this area when I graduated with my MISt in 2001—mainly due to my lack of experience and technical expertise. I did have two part-time student jobs, in marketing and as a library database editor at a research based institution, and I had completed a freelance Web development project with a fellow MLS graduate. I eventually secured a three-month internship in Europe, where I worked on a corporate Intranet. Upon my return I started a one-year Web development program (Interactive Multimedia) at Sheridan College, then took on more freelance projects. I found a job as an Internet Content Coordinator/Online Marketing for an online bank, where I worked for three years before making the switch to my last position as Web & Digital Services Librarian at Seneca College.

I pursued Web development skills and completed a college program because I believed that libraries were changing and that a solid grasp of technology would be necessary in the future—and that this would also set me apart from those who did not have these skills. In short, aside from my own interest, I thought it would make me more marketable. I would not have been hired for my current role without the technical skills I acquired at Sheridan College.

Prior to obtaining my job at Seneca College I also completed an online searching and "Writing for the Web" course through University of Toronto's Professional Learning Centre (Faculty of Information Studies). I became a student member of SLA (Toronto chapter), and remained a member, even when I was not working in a library, in order to keep in touch with the library community. I have volunteered with the

Toronto chapter for several years, and I designed and continue to maintain its Web site. This continuous involvement with a professional association is excellent for networking and staying in the loop.

If interested in pursuing an alternative career, make sure you have the skills to back up your claims. For example, if you want to work in a Web-related role, it's very easy to say that you know about Web site usability through research—but implementing best practices is easier said than done without experience. Learn how to market yourself and sell your skills to potential employers who may not understand the skills a library degree can bring. I also believe that people can and should pursue a path that they find interesting; it's important not to be pigeonholed into one specific area.

As Web & Digital Services Librarian at Seneca College, my daily tasks and responsibilities included: designing, updating and maintaining Web sites, designing interface mock-ups, project management, usability, information architecture, presenting Web-related information to staff/faculty, reference services, research, and administrative tasks. While these were similar to the daily tasks in previous positions, the main difference was in understanding the audience, as well as the overall focus of the sites. In the library field, the focus is very much on information and presenting that information to the intended audience—in this case, students—with the goal that students are able to find and use this information. In my online marketing role, the focus was very much on marketing/selling (ecommerce). While usability played a role, it wasn't about presenting information for information's sake, but about presenting content in a way that would result in action from a potential client. Developing strategies for targeting potential clients was central.

Besides the fact that I had a degree that said I was a "librarian," I really wanted to work in a library for two reasons: (a) to develop some of the library skills I had been introduced to while completing my degree; and (b) to have an employer recognize my degree. Although I did not move to a more traditional library career, I did move from a marketing department in the private sector to a Web role in a library in the public sector.

My MLS degree did not mean very much to my superiors at my previous job. From a financial perspective, it bothered me knowing that fellow graduates who worked in institutions that did recognize their degrees made an average of 10K more annually than I did. I was also worried that, without a stronger connection to the library world, I would become so far removed that it would become increasingly difficult to return (or, in my case, start). It was never my intention to become disconnected from libraries and the degree I had spent time, effort, and money obtaining. I really wanted my next employer to value my degree as well as my "alternative" skill.

I initially pursued the technical side with the ultimate goal of combining both skill sets in a hybrid role. Accordingly, it was my goal that my next job require an MLS degree as well as technical skills. I was worried that this was easier said than done, knowing that these jobs are few and far between. However, six years after graduation, I'm happy to see that these types of jobs (Web librarian, etc.) are increasing, and I can only be positive about the future.

Britta Jessen Charbonneau (www.brittajessen.com) is former Web & Digital Services Librarian, Seneca College of Applied Arts & Technology, Toronto, Ontario, Canada.

general in Chapter 11, and more on gaining technology skills in Chapter 8.) If you are interested in becoming a technology trainer, volunteer to teach classes at your local public library or senior center. Read Stephanie Gerding's *The Accidental Technology Trainer* (ITI, 2007). Attend technology workshops at your institution or local system to get a feel for other trainers' techniques.

Take a similar approach toward gathering the necessary skills for any technology-related library position of interest. Any demonstrable expertise, combined with your library background, goes a long way toward ensuring your marketability. Even if you need to volunteer your skills for a while or invest in continuing education to gain particular skills, the long-term benefit to your career will make your efforts worthwhile.

Expanding Options

Many librarians find fulfillment in expanding their roles in unexpected directions while still working in their traditional jobs. While less radical than a move to a completely alternative career, this type of expansion allows librarians to incorporate the non-traditional, adding new interest and options to their current positions.

If your library is part of a larger institution, you may be able to explore opportunities within your greater organization. Some companies, for instance, offer job rotations, whereby participants can spend a certain amount of time in a different job within the same organization, in order to gain new skills to bring back to their current job and to get a "big picture" view of the organization. Although temporary, job rotations can be a great way to try out new types of work and gain useful transferable skills. Another possibility is a job exchange, where you and another employee switch positions for a given period of time. See if your organization offers these types of programs, and if not, suggest that it start. Moving into different positions within the same organization lets you draw on the familiar while also experiencing the new, and your institution can benefit from the fresh perspectives you and your colleagues bring to your temporary homes.

Another option here would be deliberately expanding your role into related activities. Where do your interests lie? Can you add literacy, outreach, programming, or another function of interest to your current duties? Propose a project and volunteer to spearhead it; never be afraid to expand your current role. Can you then write an article or a book on your new role? Create a workshop to teach others how to incorporate some of these new ideas? These types of activities can give you new resume fodder and skills to eventually use in an alternative career, or they can put you on the road to creating a blended career such as those discussed in Chapter 4. Expanding your role also carries the added satisfaction of being involved in creating something new, and lets you grow as a person and as a professional.

International Service Learning

When I began working at Lasell College, I was thrilled to be engaged in the process of teaching young people and assisting faculty and students in becoming information literate. Lasell also has a focus on service learning, which I wanted to get more involved with as a member of the community. In my personal life, I enjoyed traveling and had visited several developing countries, so I started brainstorming ways to use my career as a librarian to provide service to others in need.

Lasell had a program in place that brought student groups to poor communities in Mexico over winter break to perform service work. I applied for and received a faculty grant, which allowed me to participate in this trip and oversee a literacy project, and planned a book drive and book sale fundraiser.

With the money we earned, our group purchased a small library collection for a rural elementary school when we traveled to Mexico in January 2006.

This trip hooked me on the idea of performing library-related volunteer work abroad, and later that year I decided to use some of my summer vacation time to participate in a project in Bosnia. Collaborating with American volunteers and local Bosnians, I helped launch an endeavor aiming to preserve, protect, and inventory rare books at a monastic library outside of Sarajevo. Since Bosnia's National and University Library was destroyed during the war in 1992, such an inventory would serve to supplement the lost cultural heritage that resulted from the loss of over more than 2 million items at the National Library. At Lasell, I now give presentations in various classes focusing on the Balkan Crisis and the widespread and far-reaching consequences of war, using Bosnia as an example.

I then applied for another grant to return to Mexico in 2007, hoping to purchase another book and media collection for an orphanage in Veracruz. My grant was approved, and the Lasell community once again raised funds throughout the year, which we spent on materials for the orphanage collection in January 2007. Upon returning from this trip, I was officially made On-Site Coordinator of Lasell's Mexico program. I will be returning to our partner sites, where I plan to continue work to benefit literacy projects.

This academic year, Lasell formed an International Service-Learning Think Tank, and I was invited to participate. This team assisted me in preparing a proposal for a new service-learning partnership. I am putting together an Alternative Spring Break service trip to Nicaragua, where a group from Lasell will volunteer with the San Juan Del Sur Biblioteca

Movil, the country's first lending library, which runs a bookmobile that visits 26 rural villages.

I do not have an "alternative career," in that I still function as a traditional librarian, cataloging books, submitting interlibrary loan requests, answering reference questions, and so on. However, I have managed to revise my position in a way that allows me to help those in need, promote social justice, increase literacy, and expose college students to other cultures and their needs. Being a librarian is fulfilling on its own, but I find the direction my career has taken to be more rewarding than I ever imagined.

Lydia Pittman is Head of Technical Services, Lasell College, Newton, MA.

Adding alternative aspects to your existing job helps you keep your career fresh without having to leave the profession entirely; it also helps you broaden your skill set and mindset in the event you decide later to move on. If you wish to expand your role, think of ways to market this to your administration and to justify it within the context of your library and its mission.

If you are overwhelmed with your current duties, you may scoff at the idea of voluntarily adding another role. Expanding your career in this way, however, requires that you step back and look at your current role with fresh eyes, at "the way you've always done it." Do all of your duties still make sense in light of changing environments and patron needs? Are there ways you could streamline processes, reduce busywork, or otherwise create some space in your worklife? As Marci Alboher notes, "Figuring out which parts of our job you can give up while remaining at the top of your game is an important step in making room for something new."[2] Work also seems less like work when it involves your passions, something you love. Even if your new role expands your duties and your work-load, you may *feel* rejuvenated and less busy if you spend time in new, productive pursuits rather than in the same old, same old, or in spinning your wheels.

Blending Skills

Another option for those interested in working in a library environment, while continuing to use their outside skills and strengths, is to pursue positions that blend traditional MLS education or library skills with other strengths in less overtly technological fields. These areas range from marketing to human resources (HR) to literacy education to project management. Since librarianship is often a second (or third!) career, many librarians bring in expertise from previous careers or education and can easily find themselves filling these types of blended or nontraditional positions in libraries. Others can acquire this expertise later, through formal education, self-study, or on-the-job experience.

Some of those who work in nontraditional jobs inside libraries deliberately choose blended paths, finding that they love the working environment in libraries and the principles of the field, but that traditional library tasks fail to call on all of their strengths. The best fit for their personalities, skills, and abilities combines both library and non-library expertise. One personnel librarian explains her decision to move from cataloging to HR within her institution:

> I really, really enjoyed cataloging, especially the part about taking a look at something and figuring out how best to describe it, to promote accessibility. I liked the challenge of putting things together and solving the puzzle. The downside was that I was (and am) a huge people person. I crave interaction with people—I enjoy working in groups, meeting new people, and

sharing ideas, and there just wasn't enough of that in my cataloging work. When I saw an opening in the human resources operations of my library, I jumped at the chance. I found that my cataloging experience, including attention to detail and organization, was really helpful. Most interestingly, perhaps, I feel like I'm still trying to size things up and find the best place or the best fit—it's just that, instead of materials, I'm working with people!

Many nontraditional jobs in libraries tend to draw on traditional skills, while at the same time demanding that librarians acquire new expertise. Those in such positions see their careers as both integrally related to librarianship and essential to the mission of their organizations. This same personnel librarian continues:

I like to think of my job as helping to recruit to the profession. I work with a lot of students in my library, so it's nice to see them think of librarianship as a career, not just something to do while you earn a buck between classes. Also, as a personnel librarian, it's fun to see good matches made between a person and a position. Great things can happen when you have the right person in the right position, and I think in a way that contributes to librarianship. I also think that, because I have the library background, I'm able to "talk the talk"— I know the language that librarians speak, what an OPAC is, what ILS means, what people are talking about when they mention OCLC. This is also helpful when working with Information and Library Science grad students—having been there, working on the degree, I can still remember when coursework was helpful, and the occasions when there's just no replacement for real life experience.

Blended positions expand your role while allowing you to remain in a comfortable environment, allowing you to draw on the familiar and to use a broader range of abilities.

Jobs that require a combination of skills range from HR librarian to marketing director. Recent ads highlighting the need for these types of blended skills include verbiage such as the following:

- *Associate Director, Public Communications*: Unusual opportunity to make a difference in the community's understanding and use of a library. This position is responsible for dissemination of information on library resources and programs.

- *Collections & Merchandising Director:* Do you find your-self recommending great reads to friends, family, or total strangers on a regular basis? Do you love books and movies? Do you want your work to inspire and improve the lives of others? If you're an energetic and dynamic "people-person," we'd love for you to join our team! ... you'll oversee the selection, purchasing, processing and merchandising of books, movies, magazines, and more throughout our system ... If you're a creative force who loves thinking outside the box, this job is for you!

- *Grants Officer (LSTA):* Grants officer for LSTA, a federal grant program targeting library needs. Masters Degree preferred, and 3 years experience. Some travel required.

(Examples excerpted from jobs posted online in 2007.)

Librarians who blend these types of skills with their MLS or library background are sometimes frustrated to find that their colleagues tend not to see them as "librarians." One survey respondent in a nontraditional library position shares: "Some people are even surprised when I tell them I have an MLS. Once, when I told someone (a non-MLS) that I had an MLS, the response I got was really surprising: 'YOU have an MLS? But you seem so normal!' I still don't know what that was about ..." In this sense, nontraditional library workers report similar experiences to those who have moved out of libraries entirely: Many coworkers and colleagues seem to find it difficult to see nontraditional jobs as related to librarianship, or to see those in these positions as professional colleagues. Again, be prepared for this type of reaction and determine how fiercely you want to defend your turf as a "librarian."

When we choose to see our field's boundaries as more fluid and permeable, we are better able to build well-rounded careers that draw on our multiple skills and talents. Whether we bring skills in from previous careers, or gain them through volunteer work, self-study, or additional formal education, we can put them to good use in our libraries. The profession also benefits from incorporating new perspectives and welcoming blended roles, helping avoid complacency. When librarians take on these types of positions *as librarians,* they draw on the foundations and principles of the profession throughout their work, and help keep all areas of their libraries grounded in those foundations and principles.

Endnotes

1. Stanley Wilder, "The New Library Professional," *The Chronicle of Higher Education* Feb. 20 2007, chronicle.com/jobs/news/2007/02/2007 022001c/careers.html (accessed Sept. 20, 2007).
2. Marci Alboher, *One Person/Multiple Careers: A New Model for Work/Life Success,* New York: Warner, 2007: 24.

Chapter 10

Back Into the Fold

I think that's the best advice I can share—no matter what job you take, you will always be a librarian.[1]

Careers tend not to last forever, and you need not feel permanently locked into whatever path you choose. The shifting nature of information work, personal exigencies, and expanding opportunities all mean that info pros now shift between alternative careers and more traditional environments more easily and frequently than in the past. Even as you pursue your alternative path, you can remain receptive to the possibility of one day moving back into the field. Keep your options open and retain your connections to the profession, because you never know what the future may hold.

Some people do end up moving back into libraries because they find the corporate world doesn't match up well with their personal principles and the reasons they originally pursued librarianship. One survey respondent who moved from vendor to library work, for instance, shares: "I wanted to work for a library to feel like I was making a difference in people's lives and contributing to the greater good." Your future career decisions depend on your own values and on whether you find that your alternative career really fits your personality and your principles.

Most importantly for the profession, info pros who move back to librarianship from other fields or from a foray into self-employment bring back a wealth of new knowledge, skills, and attitudes. Their presence and perspective only enriches the profession, which benefits from the knowledge and achievements of multiple fields. We are not defined by our job titles, and the skills and experience we gain in nontraditional environments transfer easily to traditional librarianship, just as the skills and experience we gain in libraries transfer to alternative careers.

Laurie Putnam, communications consultant, Monterey, CA, and lecturer, San Jose State University, outlines some of the ways outside skills and experience can make us better professionals: "We know the skills and knowledge we develop as information professionals are transferable. I suggest thinking even more broadly: Look for skills and knowledge you've gained in other environments and think about how you can integrate them into your professional life. I developed skills and knowledge in management, marketing, writing, editing, and publishing outside of the library world, in corporations and nonprofit organizations. Now, as a consultant, I use those skills to help libraries, and as an instructor, I help others develop those skills and learn to apply them to the library world."

Keeping Connected

Those working in any alternative field can benefit by keeping up with and connected to the library profession—do so in whatever measure and by whatever combination of methods works for you. Connections can include maintaining association memberships, subscribing to journals, attending conferences, volunteering at a local library, staying in touch with library colleagues, and keeping up online through blogs and email discussion lists. Taking advantage of continuing education opportunities in the library field can also help you stay connected and help you keep up with current issues, technologies, and developments affecting the profession. (Find more on continuing education options in Chapter 11, Where To from Here?)

Heather McDonough, Proprietary Database Editor, EBSCO Publishing, Ipswich, MA, says: "I am currently keeping up with the library field first and foremost through studying to get my MLS, including discussions with professors and fellow students about the theory and practice of librarianship. In addition, I keep up with the field by volunteering at my local public library, subscribing to (and participating in) several lists, reading *Library Journal* and similar periodicals, and surfing library-related Web sites and blogs when I can." Most of those who have moved to alternative fields do try to maintain their professional ties. Another survey respondent mentions: "I am involved in library organizations and I attend conferences and events when I can. I read widely in LIS and information industry publications, blogs, etc. to stay aware of developments that affect my company and my role in the company. I edit an LIS organization's bulletin."

In order to feed both your desire to keep connected and your success in your new career, you can keep your professional involvement as relevant as possible to your alternative path. If you have moved into the Web design field, for instance, volunteer as a Webmaster for an association subgroup or small local library; if you have moved into publishing, write for the library field or volunteer to edit an association newsletter. Think also about contributing your own thoughts on a professional blog or participating in email discussion lists, giving library colleagues the benefit of your outside perspective. Also, why not use your ongoing professional reading and online involvement to explore new areas of the field that you might wish to move into in the future?

Coming Back

Our careers as 21st-century information professionals are more fluid than they were in the past, and a foray into an alternative career need not be seen as final. People do move back into more traditional librarianship, often with a wealth of new knowledge and experiences to share. Just as those who choose librarianship as a later-in-life career bring their previous experiences to bear on the profession, those who leave traditional careers and later return bring their nontraditional experience back to the field. Our field, which has always borrowed from related areas of inquiry, can only benefit by incorporating useful outside ideas and influences from career changers.

Those who have moved back to librarianship recognize a number of areas in which their nontraditional skills and background now serve them well. One survey respondent, for example, says: "[I brought back] sales skills, relationship building, business savvy, knowing how to ask for something and how to close the deal ... any deal! *All* necessary skills in the field of special librarianship." Aaron W. Dobbs, Systems and Electronic Resources/Web Design Librarian, Shippensburg University of Pennsylvania, Shippensburg, PA, cites: "Financial skills, management awareness, an outsider's perspective (which is slowly diminishing as time in academia rolls on), an impatience with long drawn out processes, a penchant for bursts of creativity to explore new methods of service to patrons and colleagues, a willingness to make an individual effort and let an idea germinate in others to become a better service."

The move back to librarianship can be easier for those who have pursued alternative careers directly related to libraries, who have worked directly with libraries, or who have kept up their professional contacts in the field. The library network you build up by working for a vendor, library-related publisher, association, or consultant, for instance, can be invaluable when seeking a more traditional library position. Sophia Apostol, Information Services Librarian, Seneca College, Toronto, Ontario, explains: "I would encourage people to pursue different paths. I have since left YBP [Library Services] and had absolutely no trouble securing employment in a library. I

Publishing to Practice

After graduate school, I was trying to find my feet in the professional world; libraries didn't seem interested in hiring me without multiple years of experience under my belt. I found a job as an Associate Editor for Medscape to help build my resume. Publishing, I believed, would use similar skills to what a librarian needed and used.

I started out primarily doing clerical work—contacting authors and arranging their contracts, paying authors, arranging for permission to use other works (figures from journals and things like that). My position expanded to researching medical topics for a variety of clinical specialties, researching possible authors, and editing and applying metadata tags for a daily newsletter. The last six months I worked there, I was primarily focused on developing two major project-tracking databases.

After years of school and juggling multiple part-time jobs, having a regular Monday-to-Friday, 9-to-6 job was fabulous! I had weekends and vacations! I loved being in an office setting, and there were always opportunities to take on more responsibility. The editors that I worked with were very encouraging and readily available to explain anything I didn't understand. They were excited for me to offer to help and take on new skills.

While working for Medscape, I made a point of keeping up in the library world. I read library focused lists and blogs. I'm a member of ALA and got updates that way. I volunteered for eight months at NYPL: Performing Arts, working with my mentor from my graduate internship in an effort to keep my skills fresh and keep up with the news. I joined the Scholarship, Research, and Writing Committee for ALA-NMRT.

Although I greatly enjoyed my position, I was aware that my advancement there would not follow the professional librarian path that I was eventually hoping to take. With the support and encouragement of my editors and coworkers, I relocated closer to family and began to seek out a job that would make use of the degree that I had earned. I wanted to actually be a librarian, and the sooner I could get experience under my belt, the better.

I do now understand some of the rigors of publishing, which will probably make me that much pickier about fact-checking and poor editing. Considering the excess of badly edited material currently being published, this might lead to something. I think I'm more confident about reviewing, having done it from the publishing side and made decisions from there. I've also seen how corporate America works and can see business practices that translate over to libraries in terms of valuing hours spent on projects and educating employees.

Abigail Goben is Librarian I, Chicago Public Library.

think the ease of transition was largely due to the fact that most academic libraries around Canada had seen me in action and knew me. Those network connections have been so helpful!"

People who keep their self-identification as librarians also find it easier to move back into working in a library. If, no matter where you work, you think of yourself as a librarian, then your transition into a job titled "librarian" seems perfectly natural. A number of survey respondents emphasized that, no matter what work they happen to be doing at this particular point in time, they still think of themselves as librarians.

Moving back into librarianship from another field or from self-employment also lets us experience what Lori Erbs, Resource

Consultant, Unlimited Resources, Acme, WA, calls "freedom from the fear of having to work for someone or do something that is not agreeable just for the money (because I can always fall back on consulting for basic survival)." You left libraries once; you can do it again if your work situation proves untenable, if you need to make more money, if you need increased flexibility. The knowledge that you can support yourself, no matter what, can make you freer to speak out, to take professional risks, and to agitate for healthy workplaces, effective change, and just plain getting things done.

Some career changers, though, do find it more difficult to move back into the field, especially if they have worked for some time in an area less closely related to libraries. Library employers need to recognize the transferable skills, fresh perspectives, and useful experiences those coming in from other fields can bring, rather than viewing time spent in a nontraditional career path as an insurmountable gap. One survey respondent says: "I want to get back into the profession desperately. Unfortunately the wave of job openings that we were promised early in the decade has not come to pass. Job-hunting is frustrating, because in spite of my achievements I can't get so much as an interview." Those transitioning back into librarianship need to emphasize both their library background and the transferable skills they bring from their nontraditional detour. They need to sell themselves to library employers, just as librarians leaving traditional jobs need to sell themselves to nonlibrary employers.

Frustrations

Many of those who have transitioned into public or academic librarianship from a corporate job report being in some sense "spoiled" by their exposure to the faster pace and more freely flowing resources of the business world. As Lori Taniguchi, Librarian, State of Hawaii Department of Land and Natural Resources, Division of

Aquatic Resources, Anuenue Fisheries Research Center, Honolulu, comments: "Librarians could use a little 'outside' experience to make them more rounded professionals. I must admit, being in the private sector did give me a little different attitude than a typical long-time state worker. I have a more 'can do, so not the drama' perspective. I also have a private sector impatience with government operations: bureaucracy, lack of support of employees, lack of training and support of professional development, slowness to make improvements and adapt to new technology, etc."

Those in similar situations might benefit both themselves and their institutions by applying their corporate mindset to library problems. Why *can't* processes in public and academic institutions speed up? What might we gain as a profession if we were quicker to accept new technology and new ideas? What can we bring back to the profession from various nonlibrary fields? How can we make our field and our institutions stronger by incorporating multiple viewpoints and the best bits of the outside world—while being sure to keep the essence of what makes libraries, libraries?

We need to be careful, though, as we incorporate outside practices and perspectives, not to fall into the trap of viewing libraries *as* businesses. Public, academic, and school libraries exist not to make a profit, but to serve their respective communities, and must remain true to the principles and practices of the profession. Moving from an outside field back into librarianship requires a shift in thinking and attitudes comparable to that which many librarians need to make when changing paths into a for-profit environment.

Championing Change

A look at the reasons people choose to leave libraries in the first place, and at what they miss the least (and the most) about library work in their new careers, can help us change our institutions and work environments for the better. Many info pros leave libraries not out of a burning desire to do something else, but due to burnout or frustration with one or more aspects of their current job. Some still love library work but leave specifically because of negative experiences with their administration, or to escape an unhealthy workplace. One survey respondent expresses a typical sentiment: "There was a management change at the library that was very disagreeable. The new management did not value the employees at all or respect their expertise ... I never wanted to leave libraries. It was a matter of preserving my sanity."

There are common threads running through many career changers' stories, including an impatience with bureaucracy, frustration with local politics, and impatience with their institutions' or coworkers' unwillingness to implement or deal with change:

- "I don't miss the slow pace of change. I don't miss local politics. I also don't miss having my graphic novel purchase suggestions rejected."

- "I miss least the fact that librarians are often not in the forefront of their company's strategy."

- "Also, to be frank, I really loathed a lot of the politics. There was a lot of cronyism and back scratching at the expense of the library."

- "The thing I miss the least is the delay in achieving results. In the library, projects just went on and on and on. Deadlines didn't really exist and things were not very efficient, there was no well-oiled machine. Working outside libraries in the vendor space, I really appreciate the strong project management and forward movement to achieve our goals."

- "The negativity and same old same old I've seen forever now; just this certain attitude I can't put my finger on;

some of the whininess we see. The same people are still on ALA Council as 15 years ago—why?"

- "I was working in the academic library as a librarian, and, when I looked around at the people around me who had been librarians there since around the time I was born I thought, 'Wow, this is it then? This is what I'll be doing for the rest of my life?' And I was dissatisfied with that concept."

Recent research shows that librarians' dissatisfaction with their institutions and their likelihood of leaving their jobs—or the profession as a whole—depends heavily on their working environment.[2] Participatory management, open communication, opportunity for advancement and professional achievement, and a lack of micromanagement all increase retention, while stifling bureaucracy and micromanagement tend to force people out. Info pros who come back into libraries do best and contribute the most when they proceed with the intention of fostering healthy working environments for themselves, their staff, and their colleagues.

Survey respondents did miss many aspects of library work in their nontraditional careers, primarily the chance to work directly with the public, their connections with work colleagues and other librarians, and the opportunity to directly effect change in their communities. Others missed the stability of the library field and found that the corporate world failed to offer the same security:

- "I know working with the public can be a mixed blessing, but having the chance to help people in a more direct way is actually one of the reasons that I am considering making the transition to a more traditional library career in the future."
- "I do miss the strong sense of community, the feeling of belonging."

- "I like the fact that I still get to conduct research, but miss the face-to-face contact with 'customers.'"

- "I enjoyed those 'aha!' or 'Eureka!' moments of discovery when I worked with students. It was very satisfying to help them learn a new concept, and many times they would teach me something new as well."

- "I miss the interaction with customers. I miss reference questions, and the diversity of questions."

Library administrations who are worried about retention can look at what people tend to appreciate and what they dislike about their working environments, trying to incorporate more of the former and avoid the latter.

Survey respondents in alternative fields also shared what they appreciate most about their nontraditional careers. Several common themes emerge here as well, including increased compensation, increased resources, more efficient processes, and the ability to just get things done: "Things happen here. There's intensity and purpose and openness to new ideas that stretches from top to bottom of the org chart." Those who come back to library work often do so with the intention of bringing back that intensity and purpose, returning to the profession with a renewed sense of possibility and energy. Their willingness to take the risk of jumping into an alternative career carries over into a willingness to take risks and accept new challenges within libraries, bringing a breath of fresh air into the institutions lucky enough to hire them.

Some people do find that they miss library work or the sense of purpose they felt in being part of the library field—a major impetus for their return. Cindy Mediavilla, Lecturer, UCLA, Library Programs Consultant, California State Library, and freelance consultant/trainer, says: "Although teaching is probably the single most rewarding thing I've ever done in my career, I love working for the State Library. Here I help make decisions that impact library services throughout the state, plus I get to interact regularly with real-world, sensible public librarians. This is what I missed most when working in academia." Distance often lends perspective. If you feel a similar pull back toward the profession while pursuing your nontraditional career, you may find that libraries are, after all, the right place for you.

Endnotes

1. Julie Harwell, "Training Resources Manager," in Priscilla K. Shontz and Richard A. Murray, eds., *A Day in the Life: Career Options in Library and Information Science,* Westport, CT: Libraries Unlimited, 2006: 309.

2. Barbara Burd, "Work Values of Academic Librarians: Exploring the Relationships between Values, Job Satisfaction, Commitment and Intent to Leave," ACRL 11th National Conference, April 10–13, 2003, Charlotte, North Carolina, www.ala.org/ala/acrl/acrlevents/burd.PDF (accessed Sept. 24, 2007).

Chapter 11

Where To from Here?

If we rethink information work, we can blow away boundaries that say "that's not what we do," and instead with confidence say "I think I'd like to explore that." Rethinking information work frees you to improvise your responses, to create careers based on saying yes to opportunity and seeing where it leads.[1]

The move toward Library 2.0 job descriptions and the changes affecting our 21st-century institutions mean that many of our careers are trending toward the "nontraditional," both inside and outside of libraries. Changes in the profession itself cannot be separated from changes in career options for librarians, information professionals, and library workers. Wherever we go, we carry our librarian identity with us; any path we follow is informed by where we came from, by our library background and education. The following sections talk about ways to plan ahead for a nontraditional career, explore reasons for earning an information science or dual degree even if you do not plan to work in a traditional institution, and investigate where our profession is headed—in terms of the line between "traditional" and "nontraditional" work and how we can best think about our options.

Ongoing changes in the library field—the trend toward alternative employment, the variety of skill sets that can be valuable both inside and outside of libraries, the blurring of boundaries between traditional library and new information work, and the influx of a new generation of information professionals—may eventually change our perception of what a librarian is (see Chapter 9 for more). As a start, we need to become less uptight about drawing lines between "us" and "them," between librarians and everyone else. Many librarians in traditional institutions now spend their days doing work unimagined a mere 10 or 15 years ago, while many information workers in nontraditional institutions are doing what could easily be seen as librarian work—and many non-MLS holders are engaged in work traditionally carried out by degreed librarians. As one survey respondent exclaims: "Librarians need to expand their views of the careers available! Educational institutions and librarian organizations seem too insular in their definitions of what librarianship is about these days. There should be more emphasis on other types of organizations that would benefit from librarian skills. At the same time, there are many people who may not have the formal education, but who possess the skills and abilities to do the job. There are very few people with librarian degrees in the research organization that supports the management consultants at my company."

More and more info pros employ their skills outside the box of traditional librarianship. *Library Journal*'s employment survey of 2005 grads notes, for instance, that "numerous LIS graduates wrote that they are not 'librarians' in the traditional sense, but they do make use of the skills and competencies learned in their master's programs. They engage in research, aid in the development of user interfaces, develop and maintain corporate web resources, all with an eye on user needs and behaviors. These graduates report a strong sense of customer service and commitment to meeting the needs of their clients, including other librarians and information professionals."[2]

Taking some time to explore where we are going next, both personally and as a profession, will help us lay out career paths for the 21st century. A level of comfort with blurring boundaries will help us expand our horizons. Librarians tend to be uncomfortable with ambiguity, but in a changing world we will find it inevitable.

Acceptance of ambiguity goes a long way toward creating a more realistic and open worldview.

Librarian 2.0

Chapter 9 outlined a number of nontraditional jobs, and the qualifications that libraries now seek for these types of positions, especially in terms of technological skills. Moving further along this road, Michael Stephens talks about the Library 2.0 job description in his blog post "Ten Tech Trends for Librarians 2007." As he explains:

> Libraries may want to evaluate and redefine certain jobs as we move more and more into a user-centered, user-driven environment, in which primary duties may include creating online tools for collaboration and creation, developing innovative programs, and serving as instructors and "strategy guides" for users. The dilemma: What duties and processes need to roll off job descriptions in order to make room for such tasks? What does this mean for our institutions?[3]

Whether we remain in traditional institutions or take our careers elsewhere, both our day-to-day duties and our institutions are bound to evolve. In this sense, many of us are trending in the long run toward careers that are "nontraditional" in comparison to typical library careers of the past. While we keep true to the principles and foundations of the profession, we continue to blur boundaries and move forward.

Odd as it may seem, commitment to these professional principles, as well as to ongoing professional involvement, can be key to developing a healthy alternative career. Your nontraditional work builds on your professional foundations as a librarian, and all of your professional activities build up toward making you an effective professional, inside or outside of the library field. Librarians 2.0 emphasize learning, involvement, and experimentation. As suggests one survey respondent (for all career changers), Librarians 2.0 "get as much experience as [they] can. The classroom is great and you learn a lot, but nothing beats rolling up your sleeves and doing different things. You don't have to do things for credit as a college class or have it even be an official internship. Even minimally, these days anyone can publish a Web site, so go and write a library-oriented blog. Or visit your local zoo or aquarium, and see if their education department can't use some help putting together a library of their collection. You can go in once a week on weekends, and you'll likely get free access to the zoo to boot. Contact the various departments on campus and see if they have a special collection they wouldn't mind having revamped. If you like putting together reading lists, do it, and post them on Amazon.com. There's so much you can do and so many ways to share the information, and all of those you can list in your resume—so take the opportunity to do your best work."

Association and professional involvement can build leadership and communication skills that are invaluable to any career. A willingness to take on new tasks and expand beyond your original or assigned roles can take your career in exciting and unexpected directions. Working as a volunteer for other libraries or local organizations expands your portfolio of transferable skills. Creating online resources for colleagues or groups strengthens your abilities and helps build connections. Library 2.0's focus on continuous improvement and the idea of "perpetual beta" also carry over to your career as a whole: Librarians 2.0 commit to lifelong learning and an ongoing evaluation of their roles—essential wherever your career path leads.

LIS Education

Given the variety of career options open to information professionals, schools of library and information science that prepare their graduates for a wider range of positions will in the long run provide more useful degrees, and remain more competitive in a changing environment. Given the integration of technology into many new and restructured positions inside libraries themselves, library schools that integrate technology throughout their curricula better prepare their graduates for life in the real library world. While certain schools' broad and innovative programs are briefly discussed here, these serve merely as examples. Be sure to investigate your full range of options, as both programs and focuses change. Start examining your options at ALA, which maintains a current directory of accredited LIS programs (www.ala.org/ala/accreditation/lisdirb/lisdirectory.htm).

Some schools of information, such as UC Berkeley (www.ischool.berkeley.edu), do forego ALA accreditation and specifically target their coursework toward preparing students to work in various nontraditional areas. If you know you never want to work in a traditional library, this sort of program might be the place for you. But if you think you may ever work in a traditional library, stick with an accredited institution so that you can meet the specific HR requirements of future employers.

Some LIS schools, including San Jose State University (slisweb.sjsu.edu) and the University of Denver (www.du.edu/education/programs/lis), offer courses focused specifically on new and alternative careers so that students can gain exposure to the full range of potential paths open to them. If your school offers such a class, give serious consideration to signing up.

In a knowledge-based economy, LIS schools are perfectly positioned to help train the information workers of the future. A number of schools have begun focusing on information management and dropping the word *library* from their names; schools of information such as the University of Michigan (UM; www.si. umich.edu) and the University of Washington (UW; www.ischoolwashington.edu)

An Interview with Amelia Kassel, President, MarketingBase, Sebastopol, CA, and Lecturer, San Jose State University SLIS

Why a course on alternative careers?
I started my research business full time in 1984, and around 1986 was invited to participate in a panel on "Alternative Careers for Librarians" organized by Jane Fisher, a librarian with an alternative career and coordinator and founder of the UC Berkeley Extension Program in Library Science. The speakers included myself (a relatively new information broker previously employed for about 14 years in traditional settings, as a biomedical librarian and then as a public librarian) and four others—a consultant, the founder of an employment agency for librarians, a freelance researcher for a movie studio, and a librarian who had worked in libraries overseas. The room, a huge lecture hall at the University of California Berkeley, was filled to overflowing, with attendees even sitting on the floor and covering the steps going down to the podium. I knew then that there was great interest in alternative careers.

Fast forward to 2007. I've been in an alternative career for 25 years and have met many others [like me] along the way. The newest development in my career has been teaching distance education courses at the graduate level for San Jose State University School of Library and Information Science (SLIS), starting in 2004. I've developed several courses that include alternative careers for librarians and information professionals as well as online research, advanced online research, and competitive intelligence research. I also was invited to teach Information Entrepreneurship as a distance education course for the University of Tennessee School of

Information Sciences during the summer of 2007. Graduate schools are excellent venues for imparting knowledge to new generations of library and information professionals who are considering alternative careers.

What types of topics and potential careers does your course cover? Can you tell me a bit about its content?

Course Description: This course provides students an opportunity to explore new and alternative careers for information professionals. The focus is on independent information businesses and options for careers that may include any of the following topics or career paths or others that a student has particular interest in. These include:

Research
- Information Brokers
- Online Researchers
- Monitoring, Tracking Alerting
- Telephone Research
- Manual Research
- Legal Research
- Public Records Research – Online/Onsite
- Market Research – Secondary/Primary
- Competitive Intelligence
- Company Research
- Industry Research
- Patent Research
- Medical Information Retrieval
- Prospect Research
- Due Diligence Research
- Document Retrieval

- Working for information industry vendors, aggregators, or other types of companies that provide services to libraries

Consulting
- Web Development and Optimization
- Teaching and Training
- Resource Development
- Intranet Development
- Library Setup and Maintenance
- Library Consulting
- Library Support
- Database Development
- Information Audit
- Expert Witness
- Publishers and Database Producers
- Ecommerce/Information Consulting

Value-Added Services
- Writing
- Synthesis
- Analysis

You also teach a course on information entrepreneurship. Can you talk a little about this course and what it covers?
It's similar to the alternative careers course, with a greater focus on independent research businesses. This course provides students an opportunity to explore the exciting field of information entrepreneurship with a focus on independent information businesses, also called information brokerages. Students discuss activities pursued by independent information professionals (IIPs) [which include all the specialized types of research previously listed, as well as]:

- Consulting (which depends on interests, background, and skills)
- Teaching and Training

Course topics include:
- Education, Skills, and Traits for Information Entrepreneurship
- Developing a Business Infrastructure
- Marketing and Sales
- Product Development and Deliverables
- Legal and Ethical Issues

What types of skills and personal qualities will be most useful to info pros seeking to expand their career options?
Independence, self-discipline, self-starter, deeply motivated and committed, flexibility, adaptability, outgoing personality, focused.

deliberately prepare graduates for either traditional or nontraditional careers. In 2007, for instance, the UM School of Information added six new specializations (Social Computing, Incentive-Centered Design, Community Informatics, Information Analysis & Retrieval, Preservation of Information, and Information Policy) to its existing three (Library & Information Services, Archives & Records Management, and Human Computer Interaction). These can be combined into degrees targeted at particular fields. (For a fascinating look at career possibilities, both traditional and non-traditional, check out UM's "Who's Hiring SI Grads?" page at www.si.umich.edu/careers/who-is-hiring.htm.) While an exploration of the argument over "library" vs. "information" science is beyond the scope of this book, do be aware of this tension and of the necessity to build a strong base of professional principles, regardless of your program's nomenclature.

Schools interested in ensuring the future marketability of their graduates would do well to impart a solid foundation of transferable skills and to adopt a multidisciplinary approach. Weech and Scott note that "Only by maintaining a current awareness of job trends within the field will schools be able to provide first-rate curricula that meet the needs of their students and optimally promote the development of skills that will allow graduates to succeed in their career of choice, be it traditional librarianship or an alternative career."[4] If you have yet to attend LIS school, investigate how well each institution you are considering prepares students for the changing roles of librarians and information workers in today's society. Curricula, professors, and support vary widely from school to school, so don't assume that they're all the same, or that accreditation requires standardization in course offerings and foci. Consider the range of possible careers open to you and ask questions like these:

- Does the school offer joint programs with other departments? Does it offer joint programs with the specific departments in which you are interested?

- What are your options for specialization? Does the school offer multiple specializations? Do these reflect the current needs of libraries and other organizations? Can these focuses be combined?

- How well does the school integrate technology into the curriculum?

- Does it offer innovative distance education programs?

- How often are courses of interest offered?

- Where do the faculty members publish? Do you recognize any of their names from their publications or other professional activities?

- Will you graduate with a skill set that transfers well to multiple environments?

Beyond basic considerations—cost, financial aid, the availability of distance learning programs, the school's reputation—see how well each institution's coursework and philosophy fit into your potential career path. Since LIS education is now more location-independent, you are free to choose a school based on factors other than geographical proximity. (Start exploring distance education programs at www.becomealibrarian.org/distanceedcomparison.htm.)

Even if you enter library school intending to work only in a traditional field, take any opportunity to broaden your experience and your coursework while attending. Courses in technology, marketing, and management, even if offered by other departments, can later be invaluable in both traditional or nontraditional environments. Look at what related departments offer; check out the courses in the schools of computer science, education, or business to help round out your LIS education. See if your LIS department will accept this coursework toward your degree, or if they will allow you to do a joint degree or an independent study that applies to both departments. We never know what our future might hold, so maximize your options from the beginning. Decide on your own learning goals; don't expect the school to do so effectively for you. Focus your papers and projects on subjects that might work their way into your potential career path(s). Explore coursework and internships in related fields.

Successful librarians and career changers are always learning, and you may choose to continue your education (see the next section) or to earn your doctorate in order to teach in an LIS program, teach in an unrelated field, or expand your career opportunities.

(Find more on the PhD in Chapter 2.) Again, consider all of your options, but you will be more geographically constrained for PhD study than when pursuing the MLS. Doctoral programs tend to be more intensive and offer fewer location-independent alternatives, although you can explore schools like Emporia's School of Library and Information Management (SLIM), which offers weekend classes and an "online platform for course enhancement" to help meet the needs of working professionals (slim.emporia.edu/ programs/programs.htm).

Continuing Education

LIS practitioners also can pursue certificates of advanced study or other non-degree opportunities, either to open up their range of career options or to increase their familiarity with newer technologies. The University of Arizona's School of Information Resources and Library Science (www.sir.arizona.edu), for example, offers an 18-credit Graduate Certificate in Digital Information Management, with courses like Introduction to Digital Collections and Introduction to Applied Technology. Wayne State's Library and Information Science Program (www.lisp.wayne.edu) offers a similar graduate certificate in information management, helping create information professionals with the ability to do everything from manage an RFID project to develop a multimedia Web site.

We don't, however, need to limit ourselves to LIS programs to continue our learning or formal education; other options may be better, faster, and/or cheaper in terms of our personal goals. The best way to hone in on continuing education is to determine what you need to know to get where you want to be. Where do you see gaps in your skills? What new technologies do you need to master? Do you need to pick up business skills? Speaking skills? Project management skills? Industry-specific skills?

Once you have determined what you need to learn, then and only then move on to finding out where you can learn it. Some topics may lend themselves best to online tutorials or one-shot workshops; some you might pick up through self-study or intensive reading; some subjects may be taught as community college continuing education classes; some may be picked up from a mentor; some might be picked up through volunteer or association work. You might apply to intensive institutes; you may choose to pursue another degree; you may want to pursue a post-graduate certificate.

One survey respondent shares: "I have decided to pursue my MBA and I start this degree in a few weeks. I don't plan to go back and work in libraries any time soon, but given my background (humanities BA) and my alternative career position focused on bibliographic data, I feel I still need to develop business savvy to advance my career. I also frequently entertain the idea of becoming an entrepreneur, and think the mindset I'll get from the MBA will be a great plus." Similarly, you can also consider going back for an MPA, an MFA, or another relevant advanced degree that will help you either to get ahead in your career or to pursue a new one.

See what your current workplace offers in terms of professional development funding or tuition reimbursement. Are these funds available to all? Can you be reimbursed for coursework that doesn't directly pertain to your current job? For any non-MLS coursework? Research scholarships and other financial aid options, and be sure that the potential benefits (tangible or otherwise!) from any new degree outweigh the costs.

Planning a Career

Many of those working in nontraditional careers talk about the accidental nature of their career paths. Their career moves have been prompted not by a deliberate decision to move into a new field, but by happenstance or opportunity. When we move beyond happenstance, though, and take the time to chart our course and examine possibilities, we are more likely to craft a credible career. This is another reason to broaden your strengths and mindset from the moment you begin library work or LIS education.

Your institution may offer benefits that you can use in exploring new career paths. If you are eligible for a sabbatical or leave of absence, why not use this time to delve deeper into a hobby, finish that book you've always wanted to write, take a class, or engage in an in-depth exploration of your personality and career preferences? If you can choose your own committee work, why not join those most likely to give you useful skills for a new career? Think creatively about your options and how your current job can serve as a springboard for your next.

After you have made the move to a new career, allow yourself to succeed, and think long-term. When you have spent time doing the hard work of changing career paths, it is tempting then to relax into your new job and just go with the flow. For a while, this is fine, but the long-term health of your career depends on your commitment to a career *path*—not just a focus on landing one *job*. Think about how you will develop your new career and what steps you need to take. Develop new professional networks and contacts. Regularly evaluate your new path to see if it continues to meet your needs. Never stand still.

Broadening Horizons

The blurring of boundaries in our knowledge economy requires us to expand our definition of *librarian* or *information professional*—and also to overcome some of our more insular tendencies. Librarians who have taken alternative paths report that some of their former colleagues and other info pros look down on their choice, accusing them of abandoning the field or of selling out. Abigail Goben, now Librarian I, Chicago Public Library, explains:

I wish I had known how much the profession would look down upon my taking a non-traditional job. At 22, I was fresh out of graduate school and trying to support myself, so when libraries seemed uninterested and a fulltime publishing job came up, I went for it without hesitation. Over the year I spent with the publisher, it was very hard to feel like library professionals took me seriously.

On lists, people claimed to find it interesting that I'd taken a non-traditional path, but I recall being told very bluntly that I had abandoned the profession and that I wasn't a serious librarian. One poster suggested that I quit the job that was paying rent and find a part-time job so I could really get some professional experience ... The condescension of librarians actually working in the field turned me off to many of my colleagues and gave me a sour taste for the profession.

Goben's experiences are far from isolated. (Read more about Goben's career path in Chapter 10.) Merissa Enterline, Coordinator of Prospect Research, Middlebury College, Middlebury, VT, says, "I wish I had known that I'd get such a hard time from librarians and non-librarians alike for getting my MLS and 'not using it,'" while Gayle Gossen, Field Sales Manager, Thomson Carswell, Toronto, Ontario, concurs: "I least like how some other librarians treat me—I have gone over to the 'dark side,' or the vendor side." Other survey respondents share their frustration in lacking a snappy comeback to comments such as "but—you're not a *real* librarian."

As a profession, we have no excuse for treating our own this way. Not only are people's career choices their own business, but the defensiveness that comes into play and the artificial divisions we throw up between one another keep us from building effective networks and drawing on the strengths of our colleagues working in other areas—which is necessary if we are to maintain a vibrant and relevant profession. We already recognize a youth services librarian in a rural library, a metadata librarian at a research university, and a law librarian at a small private firm all as librarians, even though their day-to-day duties, clientele, and payscales differ greatly. Why can't we open up the tent further and recognize those in nontraditional careers as also akin to us? Why do we need to throw up barriers? Why should other people's choices reflect on us?

While retention is an issue worth exploring, looking at *why* people choose to leave individual libraries and/or the profession is likely to be more productive in encouraging retention than simply condemning them for their choice. Exit interviews, attention to creating healthy work environments, efforts to increase library salaries and librarians' image, and a focus on professional development and promotion can all be positive steps in this direction (see more on this in Chapter 10).

Even more interestingly, some nontraditional librarians in related fields or institutions report that only their librarian colleagues have trouble seeing their work as related to librarianship, while nonlibrarians easily make the connection. As Scott Thomson, Health Learning Center Cancer Satellite Coordinator, Northwestern Memorial Hospital, Chicago, IL, explains: "I'm not exactly sure how 'non-traditional' my job is. It seems to depend on who I'm talking to—other librarians tend to view my job as very non-traditional, while non-librarians can see it as library work with a specific population."

We talk about the practice of degreed librarians leaving the traditional library field as "wastage," rather than rejoicing in the growing need for information skills in society at large and the increased range of options available to us. We also fail to recognize the impact librarians make out in the larger world of information work. Information professionals who earn respect in their alternative careers increase people's appreciation of librarians' skills in general. As Steve Borley points out:

> If we are to thrive as a profession we have to decide to regard our peers that go off and do something a bit different in a new way. They are not breaking some oath to only apply what they know and only in pure information environments like libraries and research teams. … If, as individuals and as a body of networking groups, professional bodies and library schools, we see this exploration as somehow "the other" and not really what we do, then the profession will be taking the most retrograde step imaginable. We'll be turning our backs on the opportunities afforded to us by this explosion in knowledge work. In an era where our opportunities should be increasing, we'd be retreating behind a defensive wall built of a very, very narrow view of what we've always been. And what will happen? The same as happened with the explosion of intranets around a decade ago: someone else will seize the opportunity and begin to call the shots. We'll be ceding knowledge work to people who would never consider themselves to be information professionals and will have no reason to link in with us.[5]

Expanding the fold allows us to expand our view of what knowledge work entails, as well as to lay claim to information work in multiple disciplines rather than ceding the field to other professions.

Recognizing information work wherever it appears would also go a long way toward expanding info pros' options and easing any entry-level employment strain. If those having difficulty finding employment in traditional institutions or those in the areas around library schools glutted with new grads are encouraged to broaden their job search and recognize their transferable skills, then opportunities increase for all. If library schools and schools of information recognize the unlimited potential of the field, their graduates will leave school better prepared for careers in the broader world of information work. We need to welcome all information workers, regardless of their current job title or degree status, in order to remain relevant, to remain connected to the larger world, and to avoid alienating people from the profession they still love.

Endnotes

1. G. Kim Dority, *Rethinking Information Work: A Career Guide for Librarians and Other Information Professionals,* Newport, CT: Libraries Unlimited, 2006: 197.

2. Stephanie Maatta, "Starting Pay Breaks $40K—Placements & Salaries 2005," *Library Journal* Oct. 15, 2006, www.libraryjournal.com/article/CA6379540.html (accessed Oct. 4, 2007).

3. Michael Stephens, "Ten Tech Trends for Librarians 2007," *Tame the Web: Libraries and Technology*, March 7, 2007, tametheweb.com/2007/03/ten_tech_trends_for_librarians_1.html (accessed 7 March, 2007). For more on Stephens' thinking on 2.0 library careers, see his three-part series of posts "On the 2.0 Job Description" at ALA TechSource: part 1, www.techsource.ala.org/blog/2006/03/on-the-20-job-description-part-1.html; part 2, www.techsource.ala.org/blog/2006/04/on-the-20-job-description-part-2-lis-students-in-a-20-world.html; and part 3, www.techsource.ala.org/blog/2006/12/desperately-seeking-the-adaptive-librarian-on-the-20-job-description-part-3.html.

4. Terry L. Weech and Alison Scott, "Are Students Really Entering Careers in Librarianship? An Analysis of Career Patterns after Graduation from LIS Schools," World Library and Information Congress: 71st IFLA General Conference and Council, "Libraries—A Voyage of Discovery," August 14–18, 2005, Oslo, Norway, www.ifla.org/IV/ifla71/papers/059e-Weech_Scott.pdf (accessed May 24, 2007): 10.

5. Steve Borley, "Captain Cook vs. the Tadpole—the Captain Wins Hands Down: How You Work—Not What You Do—Makes You an Information Professional," *Business Information Review* 22:4 (2005): 236.

Appendix A

Finding Nontraditional Positions

> *An employer may want a knowledge manager or an indexer, but if their real business is making shoes, they don't know where knowledge managers or indexers "live" on the Web. So they list the job on a site they do know—a footwear industry portal. When you look for a "nontraditional library job," you can't assume that the employer knows exactly who you are or where to find you. Instead you must focus on their information universe: Where would they post such a position if they had no idea of where to look for someone with your skills?[1]*

Job hunting in the nonlibrary world may be a new experience for many librarians making the leap to an alternative career. You'll need to retool your resume, locate new places to search, call on others in your network, and acquaint yourself with the norms and expectations of your new field. (You can find ideas for field-specific resources in the pertinent sections throughout this book.)

If you intend to remain in a field related to librarianship or to continue in some way doing information work, you have several options. First, you can consider signing up with one or more of the staffing firms in the field (see www.lisjobs.com/temp.htm). Vendors and companies seeking information workers often turn to employment agencies to fill vacancies, and these agencies can keep your resume on file in case an appropriate opportunity arises.

Also, search for email discussion lists in your area of interest. For example, if you are interested in branching out into patent searching, you might want to join the PIUG (Patent Information User's Group) list (www.piug.org/list.php); if you are interested in records management, join ARMA's RIM list (www.arma.org/rim/listserv. cfm) or RECMGMT-L (www.lsoft.com/scripts/wl.exe?SL1= RECMGMT-L&H=LISTS.UFL.EDU). Look for similar lists in your particular area(s) of interest. Not only will you benefit from their discussions, but also specialized job postings often appear only on specialized lists.

One survey respondent now working as a researcher suggests: "Look *everywhere,* in every place you can think of. Although traditional library job Web sites are great and wonderful, most jobs listed require an MLS (and every other librarian looking for a job is looking at the same listings you are). Interestingly, I found my job listed on craigslist, under the heading: Librarian/Researcher." Some specialized job search resources for finding information-related positions both in and outside of libraries include:

- AMIA Job Exchange, www.amia.org/inside/jobex –
  Includes jobs in biomedical and health informatics

- SLA Career Center, sla.jobcontrolcenter.com/search –
  Includes jobs in competitive intelligence, knowledge
  management, publishing, and other alternative fields;
  also try the SLA email lists in your area of interest, as well
  as the chapters in your desired location

- University of Washington's iProJobs email list,
  mailman1.u.washington.edu/mailman/listinfo/iprojobs

Also try general job search sites such as Monster.com (www.monster.com) and CareerBuilder.com (www.careerbuilder. com), on which companies often post all of their open positions—

including information-related jobs for which they may not think of a librarian. Definitely visit craigslist (www.craigslist.org) for career opportunities in research, as well as oddball or independent jobs that might not show up on the major career boards. Think about the terminology an organization might use to describe your desired job. (A number of possible terms for information-related jobs can be found in Chapter 6.)

Beyond these strategies, think about narrowing your search even further. If you wish to work in a particular industry, use your librarian skills to locate the email lists, sites, associations, and job boards frequented by those in that industry. If you wish to work in a particular industry in a particular location, make a list of the major employers in that business and in that area. Bookmark their employment sites, locate the local associations of which they are likely to be a member, set up informational interviews, and send them your resume. The Riley Guide has a useful page on how to research and target employers and locations (rileyguide.com/research.html).

Making Your Case

Jumping to another field requires you to be able not only to see how your skills and experience transfer, but to outline these in terms your new employer will understand. While you always need to tailor your cover letter and resume to any desired job, positioning yourself as a viable candidate for nonlibrary work requires a bit more finesse and attention. Here, it's more important to talk about what you have *done* than about the particular jobs you have held. Think in terms of key words here: Your resume might be "read" first by a machine programmed to spit out inexact matches; HR departments might only be familiar with the specific terminology used in their field.

As Heather McDonough, Proprietary Database Editor, EBSCO Publishing, Ipswich, MA, suggests: "Once you know as much as possible about which position you wish to apply for, tailor your resume to highlight the skills you learned in library school or while working in a library that seem applicable to this position. Don't assume that a potential employer will know what is taught in library school or what an average librarian does on the job. Many people don't understand the wide variety of tasks that librarians perform and the knowledge they carry around with them, so be sure to explain your previous jobs and education thoroughly in an interview, and emphasize how your skill set would fit the specific position for which you are applying."

In your cover letters for jobs outside the library field, also address the issue of career change head on. Concisely outline your reasons for the change and the pertinent skills you bring to the table. Career change requires knowing yourself and what you can do, so go back to the career exploration described in Chapter 1. Nicole Gustine, Information Specialist, The Glosten Associates, Inc, Seattle, WA, emphasizes: "Know what you are good at and what you like doing and advertise that to an employer. If you have skills to offer, see a need, and know how to communicate about how your skills could fill the need, sometimes you can get the job that you want, not just the one you are being offered."

Prepare for the interview as well, where your firm knowledge of transferable skills will again be key. Identify some stories or experiences from your previous career(s) that highlight these, and be ready to bring them out in response to relevant questions. Be able to back up your claims of transferable skills with concrete examples of what you have accomplished. Prior to the interview, research the company and similar jobs (another task right up an info pro's alley!) and come prepared to display your knowledge of the organization's unique needs.

Realize that salary negotiations are more often expected in the corporate world, but bring up the issue of salary *after* receiving an offer, not during the interview process. Think about the long-term implications of failing to negotiate; companies generally make the lowest offer they think you may accept, leaving room for negotiation. Even a small bump at the beginning of your career, multiplied over years of percentage-based raises, can have a huge long-term impact. Be sure to research average salaries in your new field so you know what to expect and what you may be worth.

Retooling Your Resume

Forget the old "rule" about keeping your resume to a single page. Here, you want to emphasize transferable skills, so think about doing a functional (or competency-based) resume rather than a traditional chronological one. Functional resumes cluster your experience in groups of skills, rather than listing duties under each reverse-chronological position. (Find a useful article on and examples of functional resumes at Quintessential Careers, www.quintcareers.com/functional_resume.html.) Other useful options for career changers: a hybrid resume, which uses the same skills grouping as a functional resume but also allows you to briefly list duties under individual positions in a separate chronological section; or a portfolio resume, which focuses on describing your major accomplishments and achievements.

In any of these cases, use a combination of action verbs and specific numbers and examples to describe your accomplishments, rather than simply listing job duties. Also take the time to create an online portfolio that highlights examples of your work; you can point employers to this or link to it when applying electronically.

When retooling your resume, start by reading job ads in the industry or industries you're targeting. (You may wish to create more than one resume to target more than one field.) See what skills and abilities employers in that field are seeking; think about how your skills transfer and how you can best describe them on your resume using their own terminology. Get rid of any library jargon, and take the time to research the field and translate your skills into its preferred terminology.

In the end, your ability to research and to learn makes you an asset to any field—but only you can make yourself marketable.

Endnotes

1. Mary-Ellen Mort, "The Info Pro's Survival Guide to Job Hunting," *Searcher* July 2002, www.infotoday.com/searcher/jul02/mort.htm (accessed Sept. 14, 2007).

Appendix B

Alternative Careers Survey

The sidebars and quotes throughout this book stem from a survey posted online at The Liminal Librarian (www.lisjobs.com/blog) during March–May of 2007. The alternative careers survey was announced on multiple discussion lists and blogs, as well as in ALA's *AL Direct* and in LISjobs.com's *Info Career Trends* newsletter, and was also emailed directly to a number of people working in alternative fields. The survey garnered 94 usable responses, and targeted follow-up questions and requests for clarification were later emailed to some of the respondents.

The text of the survey follows:

> I'm working on a book on alternative careers for librarians, and am looking for input from folks who have pursued nontraditional paths.
>
> I'm interested in hearing from a broad variety of people, including: those who have embarked on a new career after working for some time in libraries, those who earned an MLS but never worked in a traditional library setting, those who pursue alternative opportunities as a supplement to a traditional library career, those who work in a traditional setting but do nontraditional work, and those who do library work in nontraditional settings. Basically, if you think you might have/had some sort of nontraditional career, I'd love to hear from you—thanks!
>
> A few survey questions follow. Please feel free to distribute widely.

Alternative Careers Survey

Thanks for taking the time to talk about your alternative career experiences. Your answers may be quoted and/or used as a sidebar interview in a forthcoming book from Information Today, Inc. If you formerly had a nontraditional career, but now have moved back into library work, please answer the questions as they pertain to your previous career.

Please email your answers to altcareers@lisjobs.com.

Email address
Name
Job Title
Institution
City, State (or equivalent)
Do you have an MLS? If yes, when and where did you earn it?
Would you like to remain anonymous if quoted in the book? Y/N

Had you worked in libraries before pursuing an alternative career? If so, for how long, and in what type/s of institutions?

Can you talk a little bit about the path you took to your alternative career? Why did you choose this particular type of work?

Can you give me an overview of what you do in your nontraditional career? What are some typical daily tasks and responsibilities?

What do you like best about your alternative career? What do you like least?

In what ways do you see this career as being related to librarianship?

In what ways have your library skills/knowledge and/or LIS education transferred?

What new skills/knowledge did you need to acquire in order to be successful? Were there ways in which your previous nonlibrary background came in handy?

What advice would you have for someone interested in pursuing a similar path? Is there anything you wish you had known prior to making the leap?

In what ways do you keep up with the library field while pursuing a nontraditional career path?

What do you miss most about libraries/library work? What do you miss least?

If there is anything else I should have asked, please ask and answer it.

May I contact you via email for clarification or additions?

May I use your answers in a forthcoming book from Information Today, Inc., tentatively titled: *What's the Alternative? Career Options for Librarians and Info Pros*?

Would you like to be notified via email when the book comes out?

If you have moved back to librarianship from a nontraditional career, please also answer the following two questions:

Why did you decide to move back to a more traditional library career?

What do you bring back to the field from your experiences in your alternative career?

Appendix C

Web Sites

Find updated links to these sites on this book's companion Web page at www.lisjobs.com/altcareers.

Chapter 1

Time to Change Jobs ... or Careers? A Quintessential Careers Quiz, www.quintcareers.com/career_change_quiz.html
Career Assessment Tools & Tests, www.quintcareers.com/career_assessment.html
LinkedIn, www.linkedin.com
Working Mother 100 Best Companies, www.workingmother.com/web?service=vpage/109
Catalyst, www.catalyst.org
Fortune Best Companies to Work for, money.cnn.com/magazines/fortune/bestcompanies/2007
Your Virtual Librarian, www.yourvirtuallibrarian.com

Chapter 2

Librarian's Yellow Pages Online, librariansyellowpages.com
LISjobs.com, lisjobs.com
AUTOCAT, listserv.syr.edu/archives/autocat.html
American Library Association Human Resources Job Listings, https://cs.ala.org/jobs/viewjobs.cfm
ALISE job board, www.alise.org/mc/page.do?sitePageId=55588&orgId=ali
jESSE, web.utk.edu/~gwhitney/jesse.html

Emporia SLIM Programs, slim.emporia.edu/programs/
   programs.htm
ALISE, www.alise.org
ALA Spectrum Doctoral Fellowship, www.ala.org/ala/diversity/
   spectrum/phdfellowship/phd.htm

Chapter 3

American Booksellers Association, www.ambook.org
BookExpo America, www.bookexpoamerica.com
BookSense, www.booksense.com
Publishers Weekly, www.publishersweekly.com
Shelf Awareness, www.shelf-awareness.com
Bookselling This Week: A Plethora of New Indies Open in 2006,
   news.bookweb.org/news/4955.html
Opening a Bookstore, www.bookweb.org/education/opening
Prospective Booksellers School, www.bookweb.org/education/
   opening/prospective.html
ABA Emerging Leaders Project, www.abaemergingleaders.org
Paz & Associates, www.pazbookbiz.com
ALA WNBA Eastman Grant, www.ala.org/ala/ourassociation/
   publishing/alapubawrds/wnbaannheidbreder.htm
The Grumpy Dragon, www.grumpydragon.com
Mediabistro.com job listings, www.mediabistro.com/joblistings
American Society of Indexers (ASI), www.asindexing.org
National Federation of Abstracting and Indexing Services
   (NFAIS), www.nfais.org
Academy of Certified Archivists, Certification, www.
   certifiedarchivists.org/html/cert.html
AAM (American Association of Museums), www.aam-
   us.org/index.cfm
Archives and Archivists (A&A) List, www.archivists.org/listservs/
   arch_listserv_terms.asp

ARMA International, www.arma.org

Aviso, Your Job Headquarters for Museum Careers, www.aam-us.org/aviso

The Official Museum Directory, www.officialmuseumdir.com

MUSEUM-L discussion list, home.ease.lsoft.com/scripts/wa.exe?A0=MUSEUM-L

Society of American Archivists, www.archivists.org

Idealist.org, www.idealist.org

USAJOBS, www.usajobs.gov

Looking for a Federal Information Job? www.loc.gov/flicc/wg/looking.pdf

craigslist, www.craigslist.org

Association of Professional Genealogists, www.apgen.org

The Board for Certification for Genealogists, www.bcgcertification.org

Genealogy Librarian News, genlibrarian.blogspot.com

National Genealogical Society, www.ngsgenealogy.org

Chapter 4

Marketing Library Services newsletter, www.infotoday.com/mls/default.shtml

American Marketing Association, www.marketingpower.com

PUBLIB, lists.webjunction.org/publib

SYSLIB-L, listserv.buffalo.edu/archives/syslib-l.html

National Book Critics Circle, www.bookcritics.org

GraceAnne Andreassi DeCandido, "How to Write a Decent Book Review," www.well.com/user/ladyhawk/bookrevs.html

Liminal Librarian 2006 Speaking Survey: Results, www.lisjobs.com/blog/?p=68

Liminal Librarian 2006 Speaking Survey: Comments, www.lisjobs.com/blog/?p=69

Toastmasters, www.toastmasters.org

Chapter 5

MARSH Affinity Group insurance, www.ala.org/ala/our association/membership/marshaffinitygroupinsurance information/marshgroupinsurance.htm

National Writer's Union, Insurance, www.nwu.org/nwu/?cmd= showPage&page_id=1.3.18

Editorial Freelancers Association, www.the-efa.org/res/ rates.html

SBA (Small Business Administration), www.sba.gov

SBA Small Business Planner, www.sba.gov/smallbusiness planner/plan/index.html

SCORE (Service Council of Retired Executives), www.score.org

ITI's *Super Searchers* series, books.infotoday.com/books/ index.shtml#sss

craigslist, www.craigslist.org

Association of Independent Information Professionals (AIIP), www.aiip.org

AIIP mentoring program, www.aiip.org/AboutAIIP/aiip mentor.html

Frequently Asked Questions About Information Brokering, www.marketingbase.com/faqs.html

Independent Librarians Exchange (ILEX), www.ala.org/ala/ascla/asclaourassoc/asclasections/ilex/ ilex.cfm

Info-Entrepreneurship, www.batesinfo.com/info-brokering.html

Online, www.infotoday.com/online

Online Insider, www.onlineinsider.net

"Resources for Independent Careers," www.rethinking informationwork.com/Independent%20Careers.html

Chapter 6

APRA Canada, www.apracanada.ca

Ketchum Canada Inc., www.kciphilanthropy.com

Association of Fundraising Professionals (AFP), www.afpnet.org

Association of Professional Researchers for Advancement (APRA),
www.aprahome.org

Foundation Directory Online, www.fconline.fdncenter.org

Society of Competitive Intelligence Professionals (SCIP),
www.scip.org

SLA Competitive Intelligence Division, units.sla.org/division/
dci/cihome.htm

SLA Competitive Intelligence Certificates, www.sla.org/
CIcertificates

ASRC Management Services, www.asrcms.com

Library Associates, www.libraryassociates.com/searchjobs.html

ARMA International, www.arma.org/careers/index.cfm

KMWorld, www.kmworld.com

SLA Knowledge Management Division, wiki.sla.org/display/
SLAKM

IFLA Knowledge Management Section, www.ifla.org/VII/s47/
index.htm

Information Architecture Institute, www.iainstitute.org

Information Architecture Resources, www.jjg.net/ia

Internet Librarian and Internet Librarian International conferences, www.infotoday.com/conferences.shtml

ResearchBuzz, www.researchbuzz.org

ResourceShelf, www.resourceshelf.com

Search Engine University, www.searchengineu.com

Information Bridges International, www.ibi-opl.com

SLA Solo Librarians Division, units.sla.org/division/dsol

MOLA, www.mola-inc.org

Google Librarian Central, librariancentral.blogspot.com

Chapter 7

American Translators Association, www.atanet.org
International Medical Interpreters Association, www.mmia.org/
default.asp
craigslist, www.craigslist.org
FreelanceWriting, www.freelancewriting.com/freelance-writing-
jobs.php
Mediabistro.com Freelance Marketplace, www.mediabistro.
com/fm
National Writers Union, www.nwu.org
American Society of Journalists and Authors, www.asja.org
Inkygirl: Daily Diversions for Writers, www.inkygirl.com

Chapter 8

ASIS&T, www.asis.org
LITA, www.lita.org
MCSE, www.microsoft.com/learning/mcp/mcse/default.mspx
MCSA, www.microsoft.com/learning/mcp/mcsa/default.mspx
CompTIA A+ certification,
certification.comptia.org/a/default.aspx

Chapter 11

ALA LIS Directory, www.ala.org/ala/accreditation/lisdirb/lis
directory.htm
San Jose State University, slisweb.sjsu.edu
University of Denver, www.du.edu/education/programs/lis
UC Berkeley, www.ischool.berkeley.edu
University of Michigan, www.si.umich.edu
University of Washington, www.ischool.washington.edu

Who's Hiring SI Grads? www.si.umich.edu/careers/who-is-hiring.htm

Comparison Guide to Distance Programs for Getting the MLS, www.becomealibrarian.org/DistanceEdComparison.htm

Emporia, slim.emporia.edu/programs/programs.htm

University of Arizona School of Information Resources & Library Science, www.sir.arizona.edu

Wayne State Library and Information Science Program, www.lisp.wayne.edu

Appendix A

Temporary and Employment Agencies, www.lisjobs.com/temp.htm

PIUG (Patent Information User's Group) list, www.piug.org/list.php

ARMA's RIM list, www.arma.org/rim/listserv.cfm

RECMGMT-L, www.lsoft.com/scripts/wl.exe?SL1=RECMGMT-L&H=LISTS.UFL.EDU

AMIA Job Exchange, www.amia.org/inside/jobex

SLA Career Center, sla.jobcontrolcenter.com/search

University of Washington iProJobs email list, mailman1.u.washington.edu/mailman/listinfo/iprojobs

Monster.com, www.monster.com

CareerBuilder.com, www.careerbuilder.com

craigslist, www.craigslist.org

Riley Guide: Research & Target Employers & Locations, rileyguide.com/research.html

Quintessential Careers: "Should You Consider a Functional Format for Your Resume?" www.quintcareers.com/functional_resume.html

Appendix B

The Liminal Librarian, www.lisjobs.com/blog

Appendix D

Resources

Articles

Abell, Angela and Lucy Wingar. "The Commercial Connection: Realizing the Potential of Information Skills." *Business Information Review* 22:3 (2005): 172–181.

Ainsbury, Bob and Michelle Futornick. "The Revenge of the Library Scientist." *Online* Nov./Dec. 2000: 60–62.

Bjørner, Susanne. "Day of Epiphany." *Online* March/April 1997: 6–7.

Borley, Steve. "Captain Cook vs. the Tadpole—the Captain Wins Hands Down: How You Work—Not What You Do—Makes You an Information Professional." *Business Information Review* 22:4 (2005): 234–238.

Braun, Linda W. "New Roles: A Librarian by Any Name." *Library Journal* Feb. 1, 2002. www.libraryjournal.com/article/CA 191647.html (accessed Sept. 14, 2007).

Brown, Stephanie Willen. "The Adjunct Life." *Library Journal* June 15, 2007. www.libraryjournal.com/article/CA6449565.html (accessed July 8, 2007).

Burd, Barbara. "Work Values of Academic Librarians: Exploring the Relationships between Values, Job Satisfaction, Commitment and Intent to Leave." ACRL 11th National Conference, April 10–13, 2003, Charlotte, North Carolina. www.ala.org/ala/acrl/acrlevents/burd.pdf (accessed Sept. 24, 2007).

The Competitiveness and the Knowledge Based Economy Executive Advisory Group to CILIP. "CILIP in the Knowledge

Economy: A Leadership Strategy: The Report of the Competitiveness and the Knowledge Based Economy Executive Advisory Group to CILIP." www.cilip.org.uk/NR/rdonlyres/ F4CF8ABA-3B27-45E5-A63E-1114CE0376AD/0/keagreport.pdf (accessed August 10, 2007).

Cunningham, Cindy. "Career Alternatives: How to Expand Your Library Skills." *PNLA Quarterly* 63:1 (Fall 1998). www.pnla.org/quart/f98/careers.htm (accessed Oct. 12, 2007).

Day, Helen. "I'm an Information Professional—But What Next?: Where Can Your IP Skills Take You?" *Business Information Review* 23:3 (2006): 189–195.

DeCandido, GraceAnne A. "Hanging Out My Shingle: From Librarian to Consultant." *American Libraries* March 2000: 46–48.

de Stricker, Ulla and Annie Jean Olesen. "Is Management Consulting for You? Part One—The Basic Realities." *Searcher* March 2005: 48–53.

de Stricker, Ulla and Annie Jean Olesen. "Is Management Consulting for You? Part Two—Setting Up Shop." *Searcher* April 2005: 45–51.

de Stricker, Ulla and Annie Jean Olesen. "Is Management Consulting for You? Part Three—Client Relations: The Key to Success." *Searcher* May 2005: 21–26.

de Stricker, Ulla and Annie Jean Olesen. "Is Management Consulting for You? Part Four—Practitioners Call the Shots." *Searcher* June 2005: 25–27.

Dolan, Donna R. and John Schumacher. "New Jobs Emerging in and Around Libraries and Librarianship." *Online* Nov./Dec. 1997: 68–72, 74–76.

Elkin, Judith and Clare Nankivell. "Wastage Within the Library and Information Profession: A Report." *Journal of Librarianship and Information Science* 24:2 (1992): 71–77.

Gauthier, Ronald M. "Librarian, Or Author?" *Library Journal* August 15, 2007. www.libraryjournal.com/article/CA6466635. html (accessed October 12, 2007).

Hiebert, Krista. "Reflections on Alternative Librarianship." *Feliciter* 47:6 (2001): 281.

Houdek, Frank G. "'alt.lawlibrarian': New Career Paths for Law Librarians." *Law Library Journal* 93 (2001): 375–422. www.aall-net.org/products/pub_llj_v93n03/2001_20.pdf (accessed Oct. 12, 2007).

Johnson, Maureen. "Jump In, the Water's Fine: Alternative Choices for Librarians." *Feliciter* 46:5 (2000): 260–262.

Lavengood, Kathryn A. and Pam Kiser. "Information Professionals in the Text Mine." *Online* May/June 2007. www.infotoday.com/online/may07/Lavengood_Kiser.shtml (accessed Oct. 12, 2007).

Longo, Brunella. "How a Librarian Can Live Nine Lives in a Knowledge-Based Economy." *Computers in Libraries* Nov./Dec. 2001. www.infotoday.com/cilmag/nov01/longo.htm (accessed Sept. 14, 2007).

Luzius, Jeff and Allyson Ard. "Leaving the Academic Library." *The Journal of Academic Librarianship* 32:6 (2006): 593–598.

Maatta, Stephanie. "Salaries Stalled, Jobs Tight." *Library Journal* Oct. 15, 2003 www.libraryjournal.com/article/CA325077.html (accessed Oct. 4, 2007).

Maatta, Stephanie. "Placements and Salaries 2003: Jobs! (Eventually)." *Library Journal* Oct. 15, 2004. www.libraryjournal. com/article/CA471018.html (accessed Oct. 4, 2007).

Maatta, Stephanie. "Closing the Gap—Placements and Salaries 2004." *Library Journal* Oct. 15, 2005. www.libraryjournal.com/article/CA6269428.html (accessed Oct. 4, 2007).

Maatta, Stephanie. "Starting Pay Breaks $40K—Placements & Salaries 2005." *Library Journal* Oct. 15, 2006. www.libraryjournal. com/article/CA6379540.html (accessed Oct. 4, 2007).

Maatta, Stephanie. "What's an MLIS Worth?" *Library Journal* Oct. 15, 2007. www.libraryjournal.com/article/CA6490671.html (accessed Oct. 16, 2007).

Mort, Mary-Ellen. "The Info Pro's Survival Guide to Job Hunting". *Searcher* July 2002. www.infotoday.com/searcher/jul02/mort. htm (accessed Sept. 14, 2007).

Neal, James G. "Raised by Wolves." *Library Journal* Feb. 15, 2006. www.libraryjournal.com/article/CA6304405.html (accessed March 5, 2007).

Oder, Norman. "Peter McCracken: Librarian as Entrepreneur." *Library Journal* Aug. 15, 2001. www.libraryjournal.com/article/CA149817.html (accessed Sept. 20, 2007).

Pantry, Sheila and Peter Griffiths. "Librarians or Knowledge Managers? What's in a Name, or Is There a Real Difference?" *Business Information Review* 20:2 (2003): 102–109.

Pergander, Mary. "Working Knowledge: Calling All Transplanted Librarians." *American Libraries* June/July 2006: 92.

Pergander, Mary. "Working Knowledge: Positions of Transition." *American Libraries* Sept. 2007: 78.

Poling, Nikki. "A Testimony to the Non-Stereotypical Librarian." *Information Outlook* 6:7 (July 2002). www.sla.org/content/Shop/Information/infoonline/2002/jul02/kitt.cfm (accessed Sept. 19, 2007).

Sellen, Betty-Carol and Susan J. Vaughn. "Librarians in Alternative Work Places." *Library Journal* Feb. 15, 1985: 108–110.

Srodin, Sharon. "Radical Reinvention: Life Beyond the Library." *Searcher* March 2007: 8–11.

Todaro, Julie. "Attention New Librarians and Career Changers: Identifying and Conveying Transferable Skills." *Library Worklife* 2:4 (April 2005). www.ala-apa.org/newsletter/vol4nospecial/career.html#transfer (accessed Oct. 12, 2007).

Wallace, Linda K. "Places an MLS Can Take You." *American Libraries* March 2002: 44–8. www.ala.org/ala/hrdr/careersin libraries/al_mls.pdf (accessed Oct. 12, 2007).

Weech, Terry L. and Alison Scott. "Are Students Really Entering Careers in Librarianship? An Analysis of Career Patterns after Graduation from LIS Schools." World Library and Information Congress: 71st IFLA General Conference and Council, "Libraries—A Voyage of Discovery." August 14–18, 2005, Oslo, Norway. www.ifla.org/IV/ifla71/papers/059e-Weech_Scott.pdf (accessed May 24, 2007).

Wilder, Stanley. "The New Library Professional." *Chronicle of Higher Education* Feb. 20 2007. chronicle.com/jobs/news/2007/02/2007022001c/careers.html (accessed March 5, 2007).

Williams, Wilda. "You *Can* Take Your MLS Out of the Library." *Library Journal* Nov. 15, 1994: 43–46.

Zipperer, Lorri. "Librarians in Evolving Corporate Roles." *Information Outlook* June 1998: 27–30.

Books

Alboher, Marci. *One Person/Multiple Careers: A New Model for Work/Life Success.* New York: Warner, 2007.

Babcock, Linda and Sara Laschever. *Women Don't Ask: The High Cost of Avoiding Negotiation—and Positive Strategies for Change.* 2nd ed. New York: Bantam, 2007.

Bates, Mary Ellen. *Building & Running a Successful Research Business: A Guide for the Independent Information Professional.* Medford, NJ: ITI, 2003.

Bennetts, Leslie. *The Feminine Mistake: Are We Giving Up Too Much?* New York: Hyperion, 2007.

Bolles, Richard Nelson. *What Color Is Your Parachute 2008? A Practical Manual for Job-Hunters and Career Changers.* Berkeley: Ten Speed Press, 2008.

Camenson, Blythe. *Opportunities in Museum Careers,* rev. ed. New York: McGraw-Hill, 2007.

Davenport, Thomas H. and Laurence Prusak. *Working Knowledge: How Organizations Manage What They Know.* Boston: HBS Press, 1998.

Dority, G. Kim. *Rethinking Information Work: A Career Guide for Librarians and Other Information Professionals.* Westport, CT: Libraries Unlimited, 2006.

Eberts, Marjorie and Margaret Gisler. *Careers for Bookworms and Other Literary Types,* 3rd ed. New York: McGraw-Hill, 2003.

Edwards, Paul and Sarah Edwards. *Finding Your Perfect Work: The New Career Guide to Making a Living, Creating a Life.* New York: Putnam, 1996, 2003.

Edwards, Paul and Sarah Edwards. *The Practical Dreamer's Handbook: Finding the Time, Money, and Energy to Live the Life You Want to Live.* New York: Penguin, 2000.

Edwards, Sarah and Paul Edwards. *Secrets of Self-Employment: Surviving and Thriving on the Ups and Downs of Being Your Own Boss.* New York: Putnam, 1991, 1996.

Everett, Melissa. *Making a Living While Making a Difference: A Guide to Creating Careers With Conscience.* New York: Bantam, 1995.

Garrett, Jesse James. *The Elements of User Experience: User-Centered Design for the Web.* New York: New Riders, 2003.

Gordon, Rachel Singer, ed. *Information Tomorrow: Reflections on Technology and the Future of Public and Academic Libraries.* Medford, NJ: ITI, 2007.

Hakim, Cliff. *We Are All Self-Employed: The New Social Contract for Working in a Changed World.* San Francisco: Berrett-Koehler Publishers, 1994.

Jansen, Julie. *I Don't Know What I Want, But I Know It's Not This: A Step-by-Step Guide to Finding Gratifying Work.* New York: Penguin, 2003.

Kane, Laura Townsend. *Straight from the Stacks: A Firsthand Guide to Careers in Library and Information Science.* Chicago: ALA, 2003.

Krannich, Caryl and Ron Krannich. *I Want To Do Something Else, But I'm Not Sure What It Is.* Manassas Park, VA: Impact Publications, 2005.

McCook, Kathleen de la Peña. *Opportunities in Library and Information Science Careers.* New York: McGraw-Hill, 2002.

Mount, Ellis. *Opening New Doors: Alternative Careers for Librarians.* Washington, DC: Special Libraries Association, 1993.

Piotrowski, Katy. *The Career Coward's Guide to Changing Careers: Sensible Strategies for Overcoming Job Search Fears.* Indianapolis, JIST Works: 2008.

Raddon, Rosemary, ed., with Angela Abell, Rossana Kendall, and Liz Roberts. *Your Career, Your Life: Career Management for the Information Professional.* Hampshire, England: Ashgate Publishing, 2005.

Sabroski, Suzanne. *Super Searchers Make It on Their Own.* Medford, NJ: CyberAge Books, 2002.

Sellen, Betty-Carol. *What Else You Can Do with a Library Degree: Career Options for the 90s and Beyond.* New York: Neal-Schuman, 1997.

Sher, Barbara. *Refuse to Choose! A Revolutionary Program for Doing Everything That You Love.* New York: Rodale, 2006.

Shontz, Priscilla K. *Jump Start Your Career in Library and Information Science.* Lanham, MD: Scarecrow Press, 2002.

Shontz, Priscilla K. and Richard A. Murray, eds. *A Day in the Life: Career Options in Library and Information Science.* Westport, CT: Libraries Unlimited, 2007.

Srikantaiah, Kanti and Michael E. D. Koenig, eds. *Knowledge Management for the Information Professional.* Medford, NJ: ITI, 2000.

Winter, Barbara J. *Making a Living Without a Job: Winning Ways for Creating Work That You Love.* New York: Bantam, 1993.

About the Author

Rachel Singer Gordon is Consulting Editor, Information Today, Inc., Book Publishing Division, and Webmaster, LISjobs.com. Rachel writes and presents widely on career development issues for librarians and maintains two blogs: The Liminal Librarian (www.lisjobs.com/blog) and Beyond the Job (with Sarah Johnson; www.beyondthejob.org). She is the author of six books on career development and technology topics, including *The Accidental Systems Librarian* (ITI, 2003), *The Librarian's Guide to Writing for Publication* (Scarecrow, 2004), *The Accidental Library Manager* (ITI, 2005), and *The NextGen Librarian's Survival Guide* (ITI, 2006). She is the editor of *Information Tomorrow: Reflections on Technology and the Future of Public and Academic Libraries* (ITI, 2007). Her MLIS is from Dominican University, and her MA is from Northwestern University.

Index